EDWIN ARLINGTON ROBINSON:
A POETRY OF THE ACT

Edwin Arlington Robinson

A Poetry of the Act

W. R. ROBINSON

The Press of Western Reserve University: 1967

For Mina

ACKNOWLEDGMENTS

A man's intellectual debts always go far beyond his powers of reckoning and his ability to repay, and this is indeed the case in what this book and I personally owe to Roy Harvey Pearce. His monumental work, *The Continuity of American Poetry,* serves as my point of departure for this essay.

Among my former associates at The Ohio State University I want to thank Jack Behar, George Colby, Elizabeth Dalton, and Professor Julian Markels for their generous aid in thinking through my subject and writing it up. To my colleagues at the University of Virginia who have allowed me to benefit from their knowledge and encouragement, I also express my gratitude. They include Professors Floyd Stovall, James Colvert, Robert Ganz, and Oliver Steele. But I am especially indebted among them to George Garrett and R. H. W. Dillard, who were instrumental in bringing this essay to publication.

I am grateful to the Macmillan Company for permission to quote from the poetry and letters of Edwin Arlington Robinson, and to the University of Virginia Research Committee for funds to cover typing expenses.

Contents

EDWIN ARLINGTON ROBINSON:
A POETRY OF THE ACT

Introduction

Comparing Edwin Arlington Robinson to Amy Lowell and Edgar Lee Masters, in his mind the ranking contemporary poets, Edward Sapir said in 1922, "Mr. Robinson is the one American poet who compels, rather than invites, attention." [1] Robinson's poetry still receives some attention today—his poems continue to appear in textbook and commercial anthologies, and he is still granted the rank of a major American poet by professional students of American literature. But in the sense that Sapir meant it, as a man whose voice must be reckoned with, Robinson has not compelled attention for some time. He sensed in his own lifetime that he was not commanding attention, and on occasion, misunderstood or despairing of an audience, he found consolation in believing that he would have more to say when he was dead.[2] Perhaps he was right, but if so that time has obviously not yet come. For some years now he has been eclipsed by a host of luminaries among American poets, Eliot, Pound, Frost, and Stevens being but the brightest. Moreover, the New Criticism, which has been the arbiter of taste in poetry over the last several decades, has almost completely ignored him,[3] while on practicing poets of the last twenty-five years he has had no detectable influence.[4] Not only is Robinson not the one American poet who compels attention today; he hardly even invites it.

The truth is that Robinson, though dead only thirty years, is a historical phenomenon, a thing of the past. But he is not unusual in this respect; it is generally true of his generation,[5] even to a great extent of such a giant as John Dewey. Since this

1

generation does not immediately precede our own, we do not suffer under the onus of its attitudes as we do under those of the twenties, and thus we can ignore Robinson if we choose, whereas we cannot ignore T. S. Eliot, whose poetry and criticism are inextricably bound up with our deepest sense of life. It is for this reason that Eliot's work is compelling, or has been until very recently, and any consideration of it usually turns out to be an ideological matter first and an aesthetic one secondly if at all. With Robinson and his generation this immediate emotional and moral involvement is absent, so we can look back at them with a large measure of historical detachment.

In fact, we insist on that detachment. It is our defense against having forgotten how to read him, and much of the poetic tradition in which he writes, ironically the dominant literary force in American letters since Emerson. While we have become sophisticates in explicating patterns of imagery and symbols, we have lost the art of reading narrative poems, Robinson's major mode, as our poets have of writing them. The close scrutiny of texts, begetting critical myopia, has blinded us to the larger aesthetic devices in the poet's repertoire. And we pride ourselves on this blindness as a matter of good taste, preferring a moral to a metaphysical art since the rise of the Southerner and the Jew to critical prominence in American literature after World War II. Our preoccupation with the past, our feelings of guilt, and those communal ties natural to critics with these regional or cultural backgrounds have disposed us in favor of dark writers such as Hawthorne and Melville, or assigned to intricately wrought art a high value as a reflecter of our intricately wrought social existence. In demoting writers of the light such as Emerson and Thoreau and in denigrating the frontier élan, with its single, separate writer struggling for self-reliance in the face of the universe, we have chosen to detach ourselves emotionally and morally from what was most natural to Robinson and the New England literary tradition in which he wrote. We have sensed, and it can be nothing more than that since we haven't bothered to read him, that he has little to teach us about matters of consequence in our lives.

But times are again changing. Though at present only vaguely honored and mute in his grave, Robinson is not for us merely another among an infinite number of historical phenomena. It seems a sociological law of recent Western civilization that a given generation quarrel with its immediate predecessor and turn to the twice-removed generation for succor and support. The twenties, thus, repudiated the liberalism of the nineties, which was based on faith in life and progress, and revived with almost unqualified enthusiasm the generation of the American Renaissance, where it found, especially in the gloomier personalities, a reflection of its own dark sense of life. The same law operates today; the attitude that the nineties is a blind age between two periods of profound wisdom has now disappeared, and it appears that this era may be more relevant to us than the twenties or the American Renaissance, at least as interpreted by the twenties. In the first place the nineties, the threshold of the twentieth century, is the source of most of the distinctive social and intellectual features of the twentieth century. Second, as the Silent Generation's otherworldliness and despair have given way to a new, "hard" humanism and cautious hope,[6] we have become increasingly interested in the humanistic art and thought of the nineties, aware that a more accurate knowledge of its spiritual features will result in a clearer delineation of our own. As a consequence, Robinson's remoteness from the present may be an advantage; with his poetry free from the surface frictions of contemporary taste and ideologies, it is possible to attend more readily to the permanent and profound aspects of his work. But because the study of Robinson's poetry is at an impasse, and has been since Mark Van Doren's book, *Edwin Arlington Robinson,* written in 1927, a reconsideration of its character and achievement can result in deeper understanding only with a change of scenery and a new cast of characters.

Van Doren observed with unsurpassed clarity that Robinson "sees life in that profound perspective which permits of its being observed from two angles at once. He sees it realistically at the same time that he sees it ideally." [7] Before and after Van Doren's book, critics, unhappy with this paradox, have attempted to interpret Robinson's poetry by giving priority to one side or the other in the conventional antinomies of philosophy and literary criticism. At the turn of the century, owing to nineteenth-century historicism and the theory of evolution, the crucial questions centered upon whether Robinson was an optimist or a pessimist, these being important philosophical attitudes because time and history were so much on men's minds. He was called both, though usually a pessimist; meanwhile, he insisted he was an optimist but qualified his commitment in such a way as almost flatly to contradict it. A poet, and therefore concerned with being rather than becoming, he revealed the truth, and the futility of the critic's question and quest, when he casually remarked, "Fortunately I don't believe in time." [8] For one who doesn't believe in time, in either a superhuman grand design of history or evolution, or simply the passing parade of experience, optimism and pessimism are irrelevant.

Subsequently, other pairs of terms have come into fashion and been employed in the same manner—and with equal futility. Attempts to categorize Robinson as classicist, romantic, rationalist, Transcendentalist, realist, idealist, or traditionalist have been equally ineffective in specifying the essential spirit of his poetry. In giving priority to one or another aspect of it, these attempts have ignored the obvious fact that his poetry not only contains the antinomies but is in its heart of hearts a paradoxical suspension of them. Thus they have been unable to unravel the Gordian knot of his art because they have mistakenly approached a "both-and" vision of life with "either-or" logic. But a paradox, Alfred North Whitehead has pointed out, signifies not a permanent bafflement of thought but a deficiency in the assumptions from which the paradox issues. Only by revising or changing assumptions can a solution be found. That the antinomies are there in his poetry and not reducible to one or the other is a fact testified to by the contradictory claims of critics as well as by the poetry itself. What must be determined if we are to

4

make sense out of his poetry is the import of the simultaneous, separate presence of these oppositions.

The first step toward that end is to associate Robinson with his proper contemporaries, not the popular literary and intellectual figures, but the *avant-garde* artists and thinkers who now loom so large on the morning horizon of intellectual life in the twentieth century. If Robinson (b. 1869) is placed among such contemporaries as Freud (b. 1856), George Bernard Shaw (b. 1856), Conrad (b. 1857), Dewey (b. 1859), Whitehead (b. 1861), Santayana (b. 1863), Max Weber (b. 1864), Unamuno (b. 1864), Yeats (b. 1865), Croce (b. 1866), Matisse (b. 1869), Valéry (b. 1874), Bertrand Russell (b. 1872), A. O. Lovejoy (b. 1873), Berdyaev (b. 1871), Robert Frost (b. 1875), Rilke (b. 1875), and Wallace Stevens (b. 1879), then the intellectual milieu in which he lived and wrote already takes a definite shape, and the preconceptions, convictions, and aspirations he entertained are already specifically circumscribed. It is possible, for instance, to recognize that this *avant-garde* is bound together by rejection of the majority point of view, characterized in William Barrett's remark, "The period from 1870 to 1914 has aptly been described by one historian as the generation of materialism." [9] All the men named above, rebels against materialism, lead the way into the twentieth century more than they reflect the nineteenth, even though born and reared in it. So too does Robinson, who claimed as much for himself when he said, "My spiritual and intellectual activity . . . are all for the future, but somehow my human life is all for the past." [10] As thinkers and artists, both Robinson and they are linked with the new thought rather than the old, with the iconoclastic rather than the conventional, and for this reason they are better understood in connection with what succeeds them—for example, with Existentialism—than with the conservative attitudes of the time.

The scene against which Robinson's poetry plays out its role emerges more vividly when we recognize the *avant-garde*'s commitment to intellectuality, a common value underlying the personal and national idiosyncracies that distinguish the various iconoclastic artists and thinkers. Wylie Sypher, in *Rococo to Cubism in Art and Literature*,[11] and Harry Levin, in "What Was Modernism?"[12] have traced its presence in and impact upon art during this period, but a cursory glance at the salient intellectual features of the time is sufficient to establish its prevalence among the *avant-garde*. Such titles as Santayana's *Life of Reason*, Valéry's *The Outlook for Intelligence*, and Whitehead's *Adventures of Ideas;* the efforts of every major philosopher, unlike the analytical ones today, to formulate a philosophical system; the popularity of Hegelianism and other forms of philosophical idealism, and of the American philosophical societies and journals that sprang up in connection with them; the innovations in mathematics, logic, and science which gave the mind hegemony over the senses in investigating nature—these in addition to the arts indicate the degree to which the creative minds of Robinson's era put their faith in intellectuality.

This commitment, however, was not to intellect, or what traditionally has been called reason, as the principle of a fixed, closed, logical reality, nor did it entail allegiance to a specific idea or system of ideas; rather, it esteemed intellect as an instrument in the conduct of life. Inevitably, given such an attitude toward intellect, intellectuality led to assumptions such as those upon which E. A. Burtt based his book, *The Metaphysical Foundations of Science:* "In the last analysis," he postulated, "it is the ultimate picture which an age forms of the nature of the world that is its most fundamental possession" and added that though "the world view of any age can be discovered in various ways one of the best is to note the recurrent problems of its philosophers."[13] Although Burtt's book was published in 1924, it reflects ideas developed by Max Weber and A. O. Lovejoy, Robinson's contemporaries, in an effort to combat historical materialism. Distinguishing human from natural history, they sought to demonstrate through a history of ideas that human history is above all the career of thought. More practically, in terms of social and political attitudes, the commitment to intellectuality resulted in modern liberalism, in belief in progress through reason and technology, and in heightened awareness

6

of the public position occupied by the intellectual. But perhaps the most vivid measure of the extent to which intellectualism was a way of life, especially in America, comes from its very rejection by the twenties, an era, as illustrated by T. S. Eliot and Ezra Pound, which could not tolerate the hope and confidence, the clarity and vigor, the faith in reason, man, and democracy, the liberalism and humanism of the preceding generation.

Though associated with this supranational intellectualism, Robinson was an American whose closest affinities were naturally with his fellow countrymen, particularly those of the Northeast. The intellectual scenery closer about his poetry was dominated by pragmatism, the indigenous American philosophy that emerged from New England in the last decades of the nineteenth century. Seemingly not a form of intellectualism because it does not give to reason, as does idealism, the power to know the absolute, pragmatism nevertheless emphasizes the power of the free mind to serve the human will by making belief and logic potent instruments in action. William James through his defense of belief and John Dewey through instrumentalism, to cite only the more obvious examples, humanized intellect by incorporating methodological realism within the life process. Neither realism nor idealism but a combination of both, pragmatism avoided their impasses by assigning the intellect power to assist in the conduct and fulfillment of life. The profound and permanent aspects of Robinson's poetry—a poetry of the act, as I call it, combining the title given to George Herbert Mead's posthumously published book, *The Philosophy of the Act,* with a phrase Wallace Stevens used to identify the poetry appropriate to his experience, "a poetry of the present" [14]—become accessible only if his work is viewed as developing parallel to pragmatism, as an aesthetic companion to its philosophical doctrines. As a poet he wrote out of the same experience, the same view of reality, as the philosopher did, but where the latter took epistemology and metaphysics as his bailiwick, the poet took aesthetic form and moral values as his.

If Robinson is linked with the contemporary Northeastern poets who rank as his peers and with whom he shares most of his preconceptions and attitudes, the connection between pragmatism and the poetry of the act, the bond between philosopher and poet, is even more readily apparent. Robert Frost, speaking of consciousness in "West-Running Brook," has a character comment, as he watches flowing water being turned back upon itself by a rock impeding its progress,

> It is the backward motion toward the source,
> Against the stream, that most we see ourselves in,
> The tribute of the current to its source.[15]

And in the well-known "Stopping by Woods" he exemplifies this process of backward motion and tribute when he moves the speaker, suspended in his course through time and the world, from a perception of the woods to empathy with them, then to self-conscious moral awareness. The poem dramatizes the process of consciousness as it moves toward greater knowledge and implies that that knowledge affects the conduct of the speaker beyond that moment. Wallace Stevens, the youngest and most theoretical among the poets of stature in Robinson's generation, even more obviously identified his subject and the quintessential fact of life as the act of the mind in dramatic encounter with reality—not only in his poetry but in his theory as well. He wrote, for example, that "to think of imagination as metaphysical is to think of it as part of life. . . . We live in the mind." [16] Actually, imagination is more than a part of life; it is the power within life, Stevens insists, for "we find that the operative force within us does not seem to be the sensibility, i.e., the feelings. It seems to be a constructive faculty, that derives its energy more from the imagination than from the sensibility." [17] Imagination, intellect, mind, consciousness, is itself a passion for "instinctive integrations which are the reason for living." [18] Contrary to the popular notion, arising from unfavorable comparison with Europeans, that the American is anti-intellectual or that he is schizoid—attributable perhaps to Santayana's *Character and Opinion in the United States* as much as to any other source—the Northeastern American at his best has been motivated by an intellectual passion for metaphysical and moral unity achieved

8

through the marriage of mind with nature. In this tradition it is, as William Carlos Williams said, "the play of the mind we are after." [19] And it follows, as Williams went on to say, that "it is in our minds we must find our relief." [20] If pragmatism states the discursive truth about reason engaged in the world, the poetry of the act gives us the feel of that life, the human-moral meaning for the life of an intellectual creature in modern America.

When seen moving within an appropriate and favorable setting with laudable company, Robinson axiomatically assumes his rightful position as a major figure in the life of the mind during his career. His intellectuality places him, unquestionably, among the modernists—or in the Modern Movement or Tradition, as it is now officially referred to by literary historians. Robinson's "return to the earth" makes him, along with Conrad, Yeats, Eliot, Stevens, William Carlos Williams, and Dylan Thomas, what J. Hillis Miller, employing a phrase from Wallace Stevens, has called a poet of reality.[21] And he moves in step with that illustrious phalanx of men who have been pioneers in formulating "unitive thought," that thought devoted to understanding the "universal formative process in every phenomenon, and underlying all dualisms," [22] as L. L. Whyte has labeled and defined the most vigorous intellectual current in the twentieth century.

Because I favor Whyte's larger perspective, philosophers play a large supporting role in my discussion of Robinson's poetry. The only way I can perhaps convincingly justify that is to confess that I am more interested in and know more about philosophy than I do about social history, sociology, or psychology. Since philosophers appear so prominently, I suppose it is necessary to protest that I am not writing intellectual history. That discipline figures in my discussion, as do *explication de texte* and even biographical criticism, but none of these are ends in themselves or predominant. Decidedly there is no sociological or psychological criticism; I make no attempts at causal explanations, at least outside the vital principles inherent in the life of Robinson's imagination. I seek only to elucidate, following Robinson's example and thereby allowing my method to

9

arise from the material, by examining the outer form as the inner spirit made manifest. Getting attention focused on the eye—or I—of Robinson's poetry depends, first, on looking at his motive, the structure and style of his poems, his major theme, and the values implicit in what his poems are and do. As every road leads to Rome in great art, so all these matters are pervaded by a common spiritual quality. I attempt to highlight this quality through concentering about it attitudes expressed extra-poetically by Robinson and conceptually formulated by philosophers who were his contemporaries. This concentering is the second agency for drawing attention to the pervasive quality of the poetry, though not second chronologically. Both occur simultaneously, interrelated and complementary. Neither the philosophical matters nor anything else is intended to be a criterion superior to the poetry. These do not interpret Robinson's poetry; rather, they are aids in describing what is present and happening on its surface. They function as a gentle abrasive to remove the historical tarnish from the attitudes the poetry embodies so that the values inherent in it can shine forth like shining from shook foil.

Finally, though the discussion will encompass the early, middle, and late stages of Robinson's poetry, as determined primarily by the internal evidence of form, especial emphasis will be placed upon the later poems. His poetry, in accordance with his own sense of life, becomes more and more itself as his career progresses; his later poems, accordingly, provide the clearest evidence of his intentions and achievements. A standing bias against the later works of American writers has resulted in our ignoring or slighting the mature works of most of them, and this is as true of Robinson's contemporaries Robert Frost and Wallace Stevens as of Robinson himself. Poets of passion like Keats or Dylan Thomas flower early and usually fade in youth, perhaps from physical necessity; but poets of intellect mature late, since understanding and wisdom come only with experience, the cooling of passion, and long reflection. It is not altogether an accident that Frost, Robinson, Stevens, and Williams began publishing or reached their peaks relatively late in life.

The poet as truth seeker

It is impossible to meditate on time and
the mystery of the creative passage of
nature without an overwhelming emotion
at the limitations of human intelligence.

Whitehead

E. A. Robinson once replied to a graduate student's inquiry about his "philosophy" by saying, "I wish you were writing about my poetry—of which my so-called philosophy is only a small part, and probably the least important." [1] He might well have addressed this remark to most of those who have written about his work, for they, like the graduate student, have been interested primarily in his "so-called philosophy." They have sought to analyze his "vision," "the career of his mind," or "aspects of his thought"; [2] to identify him with such philosophical positions as idealism, skepticism, and transcendentalism; and to explain his views on such matters as science, evolution, freedom, and fate. Although few of them would commit themselves as enthusiastically as did Henry Steele Commager when he called Robinson "the most profound of American poets of the twentieth century," [3] they substantially agree with the characterization of Robinson's work implied in this phrase, that the most interesting elements in his poetry are the ideas it implicitly, if not explicitly, contains.

It is a mistake in any case to assume that a poet's objective is to formulate ideas or a logical system of belief. In Robinson's

11

case, this is an especially naive assumption, as he made quite clear when, irritated by the tendency to read his poetry for its "so-called philosophy," he bluntly asserted, "I am not a philosopher. I don't intend to be one." [4] When he said this he was not trying to draw attention away from the content of his poetry to his technical virtuosity, nor was he merely making the obvious point that he wrote poems instead of philosophical tracts. For him, a clear-cut disjunction existed between philosophy as a rational, and poetry as an aesthetic, mode of apprehension, and he was insisting that as a poet he had no interest in the former. By the middle of his career, fully aware of the tendency to regard his poetry as intellectual and philosophical, he proclaimed in self-defense that "anything like a proper comprehension of [his] product was, and is—so far as it is at all—a matter of feeling, not of cerebration." [5] And to remove all doubt about his attitude toward poetry as a vehicle for ideas or philosophy, he defined poetry as "a language that tells us through more or less emotional reaction, what cannot be said." [6] Like William James, Whitehead, Unamuno, and other leading thinkers and artists of his generation, he regarded feeling as an ocean of being upon which the ship of thought superficially navigates. For this reason he emphatically opposed an assumption which, in effect, denies his poetry its existence and authority as art by identifying it with, or subordinating it to, discursive ideas. To translate his poetry into philosophical terms was, in his eyes, to miss the point of it entirely; it was to reduce it to the very thing it was intended to repudiate.

Despite Robinson's protestations, however, those who have approached him as a profound thinker have not been mistaken in their sense of the fundamental motive and character of his poetry. They have correctly detected his deepest and abiding concern, a concern which he revealed when he wrote, in a letter to Harry de Forest Smith, "If anything is worthy of a man's best and hardest effort, that effort is the utterance of what he believes to be the truth." [7] And again to Smith on the same matter but with different emphasis, he confirmed his devotion to truth when he wrote, "No man can have a very good time—of the right sort, at any rate—until he understands things." [8] Those who have approached Robinson as a thinker have detected his desire for truth and then assumed that his methods and results were intellectual or philosophical.

But Robinson agreed with the idea of poetry favored by other poets of his time that "poetry as verbal alchemy is a way of experiencing, never the expression or illustration of a 'philosophy.' It never begins with ideas nor ends with them. Its magic consists in getting along without the guidance of generalizations." Harold Rosenberg, who made this statement about Valéry's idea of poetry, goes on to say that "Valéry denied he was a 'philosophical poet,' since philosophy and poetry, each consisting of its own 'apparatus,' cannot be reconciled." [9] Robinson made the same denial; so if he is a philosophical poet at all, it is only in the sense that he turns his "imagination on the order of all things, or on anything in the light of the whole." [10] He indeed does that, though the problems as well as his solution are formulated in aesthetic terms. Moreover, an important fact in the order of things he contemplates is a hostility between poetry and philosophy; this hostility is a crucial truth about life as he understands it. Because they have not taken seriously this incompatibility of poetry with philosophy, those who have sought his "so-called philosophy" have failed to understand how he used poetry as a means for asking and "thinking through" ultimate questions. Missing this, they have also missed his answers to them; they have missed the vision of order in all things which he came to understand through his imagination.

There can be no doubt that the aim and supreme value of life for Robinson was truth. That his poetry is also bound in service to this end is testified to not only by remarks he made, but by the frequency with which the word "truth" and related words and symbols, especially "the Light," occur in his poetry. Equally cogent and even more impressive evidence, however, is provided by "Flammonde" and *King Jasper,* the framing poems, so to speak, of the *Collected Poems.*[11] Placed first in order in the original *Collected Poems* (1921) by Robinson himself, and thus, along with the volume of which it is a part,

The Man Against the Sky, his signpost to his poetry's purpose, the first poem is a reflective monologue in which the speaker ponders the question, who was the man Flammonde? Heavy emphasis on the qualifying phrase "the man" makes it clear that in trying to know who Flammonde was the speaker is trying to understand the nature of man, himself included. The important point here is that the dramatic impetus derives from an explicitly raised question and the quest for an answer to it, although the quest, to be sure, is abortive. The poem, in short, dramatizes the mind's attempt to know. *King Jasper,* a poem for which Robinson was reading proof on his death bed and the final poem of the *Collected Poems* by accident (or logic) of time, is the tale of a man at the pinnacle of worldly power who is destroyed by the truth brought to him by a young girl named Zoe. The poem, Robinson said, is an allegory, and to one interpretation of the allegory he retorted, "Zoe isn't intended to symbolize Life. Zoe is knowledge, and the child of King Jasper, who is ignorance." [12] Thus, in the poem Robinson put at the beginning of the *Collected Poems* and in the one that is his last and most abstract treatment of his presiding concern, truth is the dominant theme. While "Flammonde" emphasizes the quest for truth, and *King Jasper* the agony of being caught in its inexorable grasp, both reveal that man's crucial experience begins and ends with truth, in the need for it or the encounter with it. Robinson's characters are, of course, aesthetic surrogates for himself. They and his poems are vehicles for recording his recognitions during his imagination's moments of truth.

The value Robinson assigned to truth, once one takes the trouble to notice, is axiomatic, but what he meant by it, and thus what he sought to give utterance to, is not so readily determinable, for it is neither a simple nor a stable quality. One common meaning he had in mind was intellectual fortitude. When it came to judging a man, for instance, he looked mainly at his intellectual courage and integrity in the face of an uncomforting world. Of his friend Thomas Sergeant Perry, whose letters he edited posthumously, one of the most praiseworthy things he could say was, "He regarded life so frankly, and

14

without complaint or criticism, as a mystery so tragic and bewildering as to be beyond all human comprehension or conjecture." [13] Although disagreeing with Perry's interpretation of the mystery as tragic, Robinson nevertheless greatly admired Perry's ability to confront an intransigent world without flinching. His commitment to this virtue was more forcefully revealed in his remark, to Richard Watson Gilder, "I admire most your willingness to look life in the face without resorting to the nauseating evasions of the 'uncompromising' optimist. The predominance of this willingness to be honest, with never a suggestion of surrender—or even of weariness—is the most admirable thing in life or in art. . . ." [14] The practice of this preaching is evident in his remark about Browning's "Rabbi Ben Ezra," of which he said, "I dislike it so much I haven't read it in thirty years. Its easy optimism is a reflection of temperament rather than of observation and experience." [15] He could condone neither the interference of emotions, such as sentimental hope or wishful thinking, with clear perception, nor an interest in the superficial, more pleasant side of life. To his friend and fellow poet William Vaughn Moody he said, "Perhaps there is too much color and not enough light in your work thus far," [16] and meant that Moody was too much distracted by appearances and not sufficiently given to the less congenial reality underlying them. The truthfulness he demanded in a man and in art, and thought lacking in Browning and Moody, he found in George Crabbe, whom he praised by saying, "His hard human pulse is throbbing still / With the sure strength that fearless truth endows" (94).

But obviously intellectual fortitude is laudable because it is a prerequisite to another form of truth—to "the most admirable thing in life and art" for Robinson: seeing things as they actually are. According to Elizabeth Bates, he remarked to her apropos of his sonnet "Many Are Called" that "some of [his] other sonnets were written for their idea, or because they held up some fragment of humanity for a moment's contemplation, or because they turned a light on some aspect of life. . . . they did not have the poetic beauty of the lines, 'The Lord Apollo,

15

who has never died, / Still holds alone his immortal reign.' " [17]
Much of the "beauty" of these lines resides in the image of a
Greek god triumphant in his immortal, solitary majesty, which
is a vision of an ideal existence where the human spirit is freed
from all the ills that flesh is heir to. Not this idealized existence,
the realm of beauty, but man's life in the here and now was
Robinson's province. Traditional strategies rely on revelation,
a priori principles, or some other unempirical authority as a stay
against change and disorder, but for Robinson "all we know is
what appears to be." This epistemological principle, favoring
direct sensory perception, rules out knowledge of or from transcendent sources. Thus he could remark about a dead friend
who had professed belief in being reunited with her acquaintances hereafter, "I doubt if she meets them, but I don't know
that she will not. My notion of immortality, and I have some
sort of notion, doesn't include the memory of this rather trivial
phase of existence." [18] Between life in this world and any other
there is no transaction, no connection except duration. Man will
not remember this life in the next, nor can he rely upon memory, intuition, or anything else to equip him with certainties
beyond this one. He is confined to what he directly experiences
on earth, and for Robinson as both man and poet that meant
that all he could know is life here and now. In effect repudiating
the aesthetics of beauty, which conceives of art as elevating man
into exalted spiritual states free of this world's physical limitations, Robinson espoused the aesthetics of truth, committing his
art to uttering the unadorned truth about things as they are.
Intellectual fortitude, then, is a necessary virtue to the mind that
would stoically confront reality, or to the hero-poet who would
dedicate himself to making accurate reports about objective
states of affairs. This is what he demanded of himself, others,
and poetry when he had Cassandra indignantly cry out, "Are
you never to have eyes / To see the world for what it is?" (12).
He made it his business to acquire those eyes and perfect his
vision.

Once Robinson committed himself to seeing the world for
what it is and giving utterance to what he saw, then the more

specialized and complicated meanings of truth emerged to plague him, those inherent in the theories of meaning known as correspondence or representation. Robinson's desire to make accurate reports about objective states of affairs led him, in his early poetry mainly, to "hold up some fragment of humanity for a moment's contemplation"—as he perhaps did in "John Evereldown," "Miniver Cheevy," and "Richard Cory," indeed, all his well-known poems about eccentric small-town characters. On the basis of his reading of these and other early poems, Charles Cestre, in *An Introduction to the Poetry of Edwin Arlington Robinson,* claimed, "Psychological analysis remains [Robinson's] chief object." [19] By explicitly endorsing Cestre's book as an accurate account of his purposes, Robinson was allowing that the poet, like the scientist, analyzes a natural phenomenon, although his subject is man's emotional life rather than material nature. The poet dissects man and presents a report that is "true to life"; concentrating, like the psychoanalyst, on man's abnormalities, he teaches his reader what human nature is. Robinson's recommendation of Cestre's book was probably a dodge. He always refused to explain his own poetry, and Nancy Evans reported of an interview,

Though he has been called the poet of the submerged self, he says that psychological observation in his poetry is accidental. Nor is he interested in the exploration of pathological extremes; it is true that Fernando Nash, *The Man Who Died Twice,* may seem a sort of case-history, but it is a poetic case-history and the method is always the poet's method.[20]

It is important to bear in mind that in the later stages of his career he spoke of his own poetry and of poetry in general in a manner alien to Cestre's concept of his purposes. But initially, when he was first formulating the questions he had to face in order to be a poet, Robinson tended to regard himself as a dissector. His clinical distance in the eccentric-character poems hints of that, but he even went so far as to portray the poet as a biologist in "Dear Friends," an early poem where he spoke of poems as "glasses to read the spirit through." At this time his poetry was an attempt to do just that; it approached man's interior life empirically, as an object, as something separate from the "reader of the spirit," whether he were the poet or the reader of the poem.

Another thing a poet can do, given the desire to make accurate reports about objective states of affairs, "is to turn a light on some aspect of life." Robinson said of "Supremacy," an early sonnet, "The verses in question must be taken as rather vague generalities; they will not bear, and I did not intend them to bear, definite analysis. To me they suggest a single and quite clear thought." [21] This way of speaking of a poem, characteristic in the early part of his career, assumes that reality is apprehended conceptually by thought, that a thought can be a poem's subject, and that a poem therefore tells us something that can be said. In practice Robinson can never quite state his "thoughts," and his early poems record the mind's futility and frustration, whether in direct statements of its failure, in narratives of abortive quest, or in dramatic statements by people unable to touch and be touched by another with the desired intimacy and emotional assurance. Always between the mind and its goal or the heart and its desire lies a shadow. What sets asunder has clear hegemony over what connects in these poems; opposites cannot fruitfully meet and be joined. Nevertheless, they issue from the assumption that man's deepest passion is for certainty through knowledge. At this stage Robinson sometimes believed that a discursive statement, like a scientific proposition, could accurately represent things as they are, and as a consequence he came exceedingly close on many occasions to becoming a versifier. He was saved from this most horrible of poetic fates because he had already sensed that his subject, the human spirit, was too deep and too alive for discursive statement to represent it truly.

It is but a short jump from turning a light on some aspect of life to turning it on life as a whole. He intuitively knew that the latter must be his goal, but the way to it was not clear, and only misleading clues were made available by the literary taste and theories that prevailed in his formative years. Whenever he wanted to draw attention to the meaning of life he relied upon

18

light as a vague symbol. To be sure, the symbol's significance varies with the context, but its most important meaning, latent from the beginning of his career but articulated clearly only at a later date, is that assigned to it by Robinson himself when he said, "Galahad's 'light' is simply the light of the Grail, interpreted universally as a spiritual realization of things and their significance. I don't see," he added, "how this can be made any more concrete, for it is not the same to any two individuals." [22] Again, it must be kept in mind that this later statement results from refinements in his notion of truth, and that in the first stage of his career to turn a light on some aspect of life or on life as a whole meant to approach spirit, in man or in the world, objectively. Eventually Robinson will understand his task to be that of "realizing" the spiritual nature of things, himself mainly, in the mind or consciousness; that is, he will employ the mind or consciousness as an ancillary vehicle for allowing the spirit to rise from its hidden, dark depths into the surface light. To begin with, however, before spirit is brought openly before the mind, the meaning of life has to be grasped by the observer, reflective intellect, as he implied in his criticism of John Donne, who, he said, "is dogmatic and ancient, and hardly to be considered as apart from his period—which is, to my mind, sufficient damnation for any writer—particularly a poet, who must be, if he is to be anything, an interpreter of life." [23] To interpret life—that finally is the poet's task as Robinson originally conceived it. For him, to interpret life was to determine its whole meaning, not just dissect or fasten upon a limited area of it. Only when life is so understood can a man have a "good time"; only then can the vital distress of existence be relieved.

Robinson can and does tell the grim truth about the adamantly antispiritual world at the same time that his poetry gives the spirit opportunity for "realization," though the emphasis ultimately must fall, by virtue of his being a poet, on the truth of the spirit. He tells two truths simultaneously, as indeed all poets do. Dwelling as it does at the crossways of the world and spirit, poetry cannot tell the one truth without at least implying the other. But the tension between the world and spirit in Robinson's poetry does not result simply from human nature. All the notions of truth he entertained at the beginning of his career have in common a strained dichotomy on the epistemological level between subject and object and, on the psychological level, between thought and being. This dichotomy is one facet in a pervasive dualism he inherited from, and identified with, materialism. Despite the efforts of Emerson, Thoreau, and Whitman to arrive at a transcendental synthesis, by the nineties materialism had divided man in two or rendered him, as a vital and a spiritual being, either an impossibility or an outcast from the world. The primary intellectual fact of life which Robinson inherited, consequently, was a split world. From this schizoid condition he derived his original sense of life. Inevitably, his primary motive also came from this division. "I have been slowly getting rid of materialism for the past year or two," [24] he said early in his career; about midway he said, concerning "The Man Against the Sky," "My purpose was to cheer people up and incidentally to indicate the futility of materialism as a thing to live by—even assuming the possible monstrous negation of having to die by it"; [25] and toward the end, having gotten rid of materialism, he said, "My philosophy . . . is mostly a statement of my inability to accept a mechanistic interpretation of the universe and life." [26] To be rid of materialism, to escape its debilitating effects in so dividing man that he becomes an object himself, to free life and the spirit from the choking bonds of a mechanistic interpretation of the universe—that was Robinson's initial and enduring problem.

The truth was his way to live with the materialistic predicament as well as to escape it. But before the truth makes him free, he and his poetry suffer adversely from, and almost succumb to, the pressure of reality, to use Wallace Stevens' phrase. So great was this pressure that, like Robert Frost and the traditional classicist, he could do little more than resign himself to the bleak burden of life. All he had left as a man and artist was his awareness, made possible by the stoic virtues of intellectual courage and honesty. Life was all too real; external conditions were an intransigent ending to all the heart's aspirations. The best he could manage was a grim laugh at poor fools like Miniver Cheevy who dared to dream or aspire.

Had Robinson accepted as final the division between mind and reality he inherited from materialism, his poetry would probably have stopped with *The Town Down the River* (1910). But truth was an obsession for him, not because he possessed and was set on promulgating it, but because it was a profound need and because it was, as the philosopher might say, problematic. Robinson's efforts to see the world as it actually is were, for this reason, as much a search for the right idea of truth as they were for truth itself.

This distinction becomes clear when we understand that truth, outside any dogmatic epistemological principles, is the relation that holds between the mind and its subject. Truth was problematic for Robinson, and his career is obviously a quest for it, because materialism so alienated the mind from spirit, so divided man's consciousness from his spiritual being, that only a new definition of the mind's relation to existence could make life and art viable. Robinson consistently writes an intellectual poetry, assuming the perspective of mind on spirit, but he is motivated to avoid an initial segregation and bring the mind into a complementary, affirmative stance before spirit. His intellectual life, viewed biographically, moves toward reconciling his mind, or theoretical ideas, with his practice, the actual impulses and laws inherent in the life of his imagination. Aesthetically, he originally believed he must grasp life assertively with the mind, but as a poet his imagination, though bound to the mind's perspective, knew more than could be discursively told, so he had to seek out a more intimate connection between head and heart. Truth was a profound need for Robinson, therefore, because materialism defined the relation between the mind and its subject in such a way as to tear man and the world apart in a debilitating dualism that could be remedied only by a radically new bond between thought and being.

The initial predicament which Robinson inherited with materialism is perhaps most explicitly stated in "Maya," which reads:

21

Through the ascending emptiness of night,
Leaving the flesh and the complacent mind
Together in their sufficiency behind,
The soul of man went up to a far height;
And where those others would have had no sight
Or sense of else than terror for the blind,
Soul met the Will, and again consigned
To the supreme illusion which is right.

"And what goes on up there," the Mind inquired
"That I know not already to be true?"—
"More than enough, but not enough for you,"
Said the descending Soul: "Here in the dark,
Where you are least revealed when most admired,
You may still be the bellows and the spark."   [871]

Here the Mind is mockingly taunted for its vanity and limitations by the enlightened Soul. Although the point of view in Robinson's poetry is usually that of the Mind rather than the Soul, nevertheless this poem characteristically takes the dichotomy between them as an established fact. The Mind's arrogance and the Soul's contempt produce an unmitigable hostility.

Here and throughout his poetry, even in the early poems in which eccentric small-town characters seem to be analyzed, the predicament is the same one that engaged the attention of *avant-garde* artists and thinkers during the nineties and that the Indian philosopher Sarvipelli Radhakrisnan described by saying,

Eastern and Western peoples are tackling the same problem, the reconciliation of the values of the mind with those of spirit. The tension between the two constitutes the meaning and purpose of history. Whether in the East or in the West, we have unresolved contradictions and attempts to solve them, to learn from each other and adapt the inheritance of the past to new and ever-changing conditions and reshape it into a new and living pattern. It is in the striving to overcome the tension between the values of spirit and the achievements of mind that we find the incomparable soaring of the human spirit and the opening of new horizons.[27]

Obviously Robinson was not concerned with a merely personal, local, or social problem but with the crux of life in his time.

His task, if he were to succeed in overcoming materialism,

was to integrate Mind and Soul. The major difficulties in determining what he meant by truth come from the fact that his "epistemological" notions about the way the mind is related to its subject undergo refinement as he progressively achieves that integration during his career. Moreover, these refinements are announced not so much in direct statement as through aesthetic devices such as point of view and narrative structure; they are achieved aesthetically, formally and narratively, rather than logically. But before we examine the aesthetic and positive means he employed to bring about that integration, a discussion of his attitude toward philosophy will help to clarify his final strategies for giving utterance to the truth.

Philosophy as traditionally conceived, and as understood by Robinson, has been our foremost intellectual instrument for determining the meaning of life in modern times, replacing the mythological and religious modes that prevailed in prerationalistic eras. But if in the bitter dialogue between Mind and Soul the Mind cannot know the Will, then the Mind cannot attain a spiritual realization of things and their significance, and philosophy as traditionally practiced is useless in determining Truth. In a letter to Will Durant, written in 1931, and therefore expressing his mature opinion, Robinson vigorously asserts that this is the case. "It is true," he wrote,

that we have acquired a great deal of material knowledge in recent years, but so far as knowledge of the truth itself is concerned, I cannot see that we are any nearer to it now than our less imaginative ancestors were when they cracked each others' skulls with stone hatchets, or that we know any more than they knew of what happened to the soul that escaped in the process. It is easy, and just now rather fashionable, to say that there is no soul, but we do not know whether there is a soul or not. If a man is a materialist, or a mechanist, . . . I can see for him no escape from belief in a futility so prolonged and complicated and diabolical and preposterous as to be worse than absurd; and as I do not know that such a tragic absurdity is not a fact, I can only know my native inability to believe that it is one . . . if life is only what it appears to be, no amount of improvement or enlightenment will ever compensate or atone for what it has inflicted and endured for ages past, or for what it is inflicting and enduring today. . . . Our teleological endowment

23

spares most of us from disturbing ourselves unduly over the freedom of the will. There is apparently not much that anyone can do about it except to follow his own light—which may or may not be an ignis fatuus in a swamp . . . the modern "mechanist" is not entirely unlike . . . an intrepid explorer standing on a promontory in a fog, looking through the newest thing in the way of glasses for an ocean that he cannot see, and shouting to his mechanistic friends behind him that he has found the end of the world.

These remarks . . . are more the result of observation and reflection than of personal discomfort and dissatisfaction. As lives go, my own life would be called, and properly, a rather fortunate one.[28]

The most noteworthy feature of this letter is how much it denies and how little it asserts. Besides admitting that his own life provides no grounds for complaint, Robinson is certain only of his native inability to believe that life is a tragic absurdity. He suggests that all one can do to counter the possibility that it may be is to follow his own light; but since the truth or falsity of that light is indeterminable, his trust in it is a matter of faith, not of intellectual certainty. The rest of the letter is outright and complete denial—knowledge of the Truth has not progressed an inch since the origin of man: we know nothing at all about final matters; materialists are myopic fools who mistakenly regard their ignorance as reality; life, judging by appearances, is brutal and meaningless. A letter deliberately designed to provoke a defense of his philosophical position evokes from Robinson a repudiation of philosophy and the meager positive claim that man can know for certain only his own feelings.

These attitudes are dramatically rendered in "Ponce de Leon." De Leon, on his death bed, asks of the doctor attending him, "Tell me something, / Tell me—what does life mean?"

> "Some of it means,
> My Lord," the old man answered, easily,
> "That hidden voices are in some of us,
> And, when we least would hear them, whisper to us
> That we had better go the other way.
> And other voices are in some of us,
> Telling us to go on as we are going—
> So long as we go sensibly and fairly,

> And with a vigilance. There are voices also,
> Saying that if this world is only this,
> We are remarkable animate accidents,
> And are all generated for a most
> Remorseless and extravagant sacrifice
> To an insatiate God of nothing at all—
> Who is not mine, or yours. And there are voices
> Coming so far to find us that I doubt
> If you, my lord, have yet an ear to seize them.
> They may be near you now, unrecognized,
> If not unwelcome, and like unseen strangers
> In a dark vestibule, saying in vain
> That they are always there. You cannot listen
> To more than you can hear; you cannot measure
> More than is yours to comprehend."   [1197]

After an exchange of words that are personal and not to the point, De Leon replies:

> "There are voices,
> Doctor, which I am glad you do not hear.
> And I am glad your eyes are watching me.
> They say more than you told me. Without them,
> Your words might have crumbled, or been lost
> In that long sound down there of broken water,
> Where you found hope. I can see more in them
> Than I can see in all the sixty years
> That I have lived. I don't say what it is;
> I don't know what it is; and shall not ask—
> So long as it is there. It may be voices."   [1198]

Obviously this passage is not much more than a dramatic statement of what Robinson said in his letter to Will Durant. Each man is bound by his readiness to perceive, by his own light or voice, and the doctor and De Leon know only that they cannot disbelieve. The point to be made about the poem is that, despite the miniscule novelty it introduces, it dramatizes two men's pondering of the ultimate question at a moment of crisis, and they can derive from their reflections only a realization of man's ignorance and a hope that a dim emotion will ultimately redeem them. What they know, if they can be said to know anything, is something they feel, not something they can conceive or articulate.

25

The general anti-intellectualism of "Ponce de Leon" is directly turned upon philosophy in the "The Burning Book: or The Contented Metaphysician." The philosopher

> has come to the end of his words
>   And alone he rejoices
> In the choiring that silence affords
>   Of ineffable voices.

> To a realm that his words may not reach
>   He may lead none to find him;
> An adept, and with nothing to teach,
>   He leaves nothing behind him.
> For the rest, he will have his release,
>   And his embers, attended
> By the large and unclamoring peace
>   Of a dream that is ended.   [48]

He discovers the impotence and folly of his aspiration to know reality via reason, his enlightenment being not the fulfillment of reason but the transcendence of it into the realm of ineffable voices.

When Robinson became exasperated by attempts to find a philosophy in his poetry and denied that he was a philosopher, clearly he was expressing a deeply felt and carefully considered opinion about the relation of philosophy to poetry. His poetry, especially after *The Town Down the River,* contains no philosophy or ideas as he understood these categories. So he was able to say, "There is no 'philosophy' in my poetry beyond an implication of an ordered universe and a sort of negation of the general futility that appears to be the basis of rational thought." [29] Rational thought, so far as he could see, is incapable of determining any order in the universe and therefore of comprehending man's being and destiny. Thus he concurred with a remark of his friend Thomas Sergeant Perry, which he remembered and obviously liked: "Philosophy is at best and highest the attempt of someone to tell me what he doesn't know." [30] And that is just what the Mind tells in Robinson's poetry—what it doesn't know about the spiritual significance of things.

The light of poetry

Time and space are but physiological
colors the eye makes, but the soul is
light.

Emerson

"Everything has stopped for the time being," Robinson
wrote to Harry de Forest Smith, in 1898, "and I am chiefly
occupied in trying to figure out how long I can hold myself up
on a foundation of abstractions." [1] He could not for long, as his
attitude toward philosophy reveals. Abstractions could not sustain him, yet he confessed, "I have always had [a light] to keep
me going." [2] This light was poetry. The most vivid fact in his
outwardly colorless life is the length to which he went to be a
poet, fighting his town, his culture, and his conscience, and for
many years suffering from poverty, guilt, neglect, and estrangement. To write his kind of poetry under the conditions he
needed to be able to write it, he turned down jobs or quit them
after short periods and refused to do hack work or to alter a
poem to suit an editor. Painfully aware of the cost of being a
poet, he jokingly advised a friend not to let his child become
one; [3] but when he was serious he would say, as he did to Edith
Isaacs, who proposed doing a biography of him, "Make clear to
those people who say that I gave up great things to write poetry,
that there was only one thing in all the world I could give up,
and that was all that meant anything to me." [4] To him, poetry—to paraphrase Santayana—was a way of living, and the
most vital way.

Having disqualified philosophy as an instrument of truth,

Robinson was free to turn to poetry, which as a poet he naturally favored anyway, though he did try fiction first and found it unamenable to his talent or purpose. But none of his poems ever discursively states the truth; he was not able to make poetry accomplish philosophically more than philosophy itself could. A very serious consequence for Robinson's poetry followed from his declaring the mind impotent. Stripped of intellectual foundations, and thrown back upon itself, Robinson's imagination had to rely solely upon its special powers, or upon the very select encounter the Soul has with the Will. Hart Crane aptly stated this predicament in a reply to a criticism that his poetry was deficient in intellectual knowledge:

The tragic quandary (or *agon*) of the modern world derives from the paradoxes that an inadequate system of rationality forces on the living consciousness. I am not opposing any new synthesis of reasonable laws which might provide a consistent philosophical and moral program for our epoch. Neither am I attempting to delineate any such system. If this "knowledge" were sufficiently organized as to dominate the limitations of my experience, then I would probably find myself writing under the "classic" power and under the circumstance might be philosophically contained.[5]

Since this knowledge is not sufficiently organized, it follows that

poetry, in so far as the metaphysics of absolute truth extends, is simply the concrete *evidence* of the *experience* of a recognition (*knowledge* if you like) . . . poetry, without attempting to logically enunciate such a problem as man's relationship to a hypothetical god or its solution, may well give us the real connective experience, the very "sign manifest" on which rests the assumption of a godhead.[6]

Robinson discovered, as Crane did at a later date, that his experience did not include an intellectual content. There was no existential ground on which to generalize or to formulate a grand scheme, and like any genuine artist he could only be true to his experience and give his art the shape of his consciousness.

The ineluctably real for him, once thought had been disqualified, was therefore the connective experience. It was the only absolutely certain datum, also, for William James, who claimed that the world of our experience consists at all times of two parts, an objective and a subjective part, of which the former may be incalculably more extensive than the latter, and yet the latter can never be omitted or suppressed. The objective part is the sum total of whatsoever at any given time we may be thinking of, the subjective part is the inner "state" in which the thinking comes to pass. What we think of may be enormous—the cosmic times and spaces, for example—whereas the inner state may be the most fugitive and paltry activity of mind. Yet the cosmic objects, so far as the experience yields them, are but ideal pictures of something whose existence we do not inwardly possess but only point at outwardly, while the inner state is our very experience itself; its reality and that of our experience are one. A conscious field plus its object as felt or thought of plus an attitude towards the object plus the sense of a self to whom the attitude belongs—such a concrete bit of personal experience may be a small bit, but it is a solid bit as long as it lasts; not hollow, not a mere abstract element of experience, such as the "object" is when taken all alone. It is of the kind to which all realities whatsoever must belong; the motor currents of the world run through the like of it; it is on the line connecting real events with real events. That unsharable feeling which each one of us has of the pinch of his individual destiny as he privately feels it rolling out on fortune's wheel may be disparaged for its egotism, may be sneered at as unscientific, but it is the one thing that fills up the measure of our concrete actuality.[7]

The mind's inequatability with the inner state of our very experience was obviously a widely recognized fact of life. Therefore not only philosophy but poetry as well was in a predicament that disqualified it for determining the objective, universal meaning of life. The imagination did not, and could not, existentially perceive a rational order in itself or the world. The light of poetry was not an all-powerful beam.

Accordingly, as Robinson's expectations of understanding life waned, the power of poetry, at least to serve the purposes of the mind, diminished for him. In the early portion of his career he was inclined to make general and grand claims for poetry, as he did in "L'Envoi":

Now in a thought, now in a shadowed word,
Now in a voice that thrills eternity,
Ever there comes an onward phrase to me

Of some transcendent music I have heard;
No piteous thing by soft hands dulcimered,
No trumpet crash of blood-sick victory,
But a glad strain of some vast harmony
That no brief mortal touch has ever stirred.

There is no music in the world like this,
No character wherewith to set it down,
No kind of instrument to make it sing.
No kind of instrument? Ah, yes, there is;
And after time and place are overthrown,
God's touch will keep its one chord quivering.
[108–109]

An early poem, "L'Envoi" attributes to poetry the power to transcend time and place, assigning it a permanence near to immortality and at least superior to history.

"Captain Craig," also of this period, is loaded with reflections on poetry, and, in fact, the entire poem can be read as an apology for it. The protagonist remarks at one point,

"But with a few good glimpses I have had
Of heaven through the little holes in hell,
I can half understand what price it is
The poet pays, at one time and another,
For those indemnifying interludes
That are to be the kernel in what lives
To shrine him when the new-born men come singing."
[133–134]

The poet, here, is an exceptional man with a special gift for higher truth who, though now he is ostracized because of his gift, will one day be a hero to a wise society. Like Yeats's golden bird, he knows things past, passing, and to come. In the most extravagant claim he ever made for the power of poetry, Robinson, through Captain Craig, expands even further on this attitude:

"The man of Galilee (or, if you choose,
The men who made the saying of the man)
Like Buddha, and the others who have seen,
Was to men's loss the Poet—though it be
The Poet only of him we revere,

30

> The Poet we remember. We have put
> The prose of him so far away from us,
> The fear of him so crudely over us,
> That I have wondered—wondered." [147]

Though Captian Craig voices some doubts about the beneficial effects of these particular poets because they have been deified (when their word becomes doctrine, it is corrupted), in referring to the great religious figures as Poets, he makes the poet a sage who sees with superhuman ability beyond the fallen world and brings the redeeming light into its darkness.

By the time Robinson wrote *Van Zorn* (1914), originally titled "Ferguson's Ivory Tower" and devoted explicitly to examining the artist's role, his notions about the power of poetry had begun to change. In it Farnsworth, a painter, is told by Van Zorn, a sage of sorts, "It is your age, Farnsworth, and you had better not play with it. If I were you I should try to meet it half way." [8] No longer can the artist stand outside the community, superior to it in wisdom, waiting for it to come around to acknowledging him and his vision. He must enter into the community's life, the world of the present, and view things in part from its perspective and serve it directly. This does not mean that art must become popular; it means, instead, that the artist is caught up in history and can produce genuine art only if he is *engaged*—which he inescapably is anyway. Another indication of poetry's diminished status at this point is the unsympathetic treatment Robinson gives to his artist characters, beginning with Farnsworth. The one possible exception is Fernando Nash, of *The Man Who Died Twice,* a musician who has a mystical experience, but his experience has a bad effect on his art, for he destroys what he has composed and composes nothing new. Umfraville, in *Roman Bartholow,* remarks, "If a true artist must go to the devil, / What's left of truth in him should keep the devil/Out of his art" (836). But Fernando Nash had been many kinds of artist and none of them had saved him; he could not, moreover, keep the devil out of his art, much less himself. In *Amaranth,* a number of artists in addition to the main character, Fargo, have exposed the vanity and limitations of their self-exaltation. From *Van Zorn* on, the artist's weaknesses —his pride, his grandiose aspirations, his contempt for the world—rather than his powers are most conspicuous. He can't keep the devil out of his art for the simple reason that, being trapped in time, his vision is necessarily corrupted. A product of the individual consciousness, poetry is always limited by a finite moment, place, and perspective. Only the humility resulting from recognition and acceptance of his human limitations can save a poet from complete folly. The poet sails in the same boat as the Flying Dutchman:

> Unyielding in the pride of his defiance,
>   Afloat with none to serve or to command,
> Lord of himself at last, and all by Science,
>   He seeks the Vanished Land.
>
> Alone, by the one light of his one thought,
>   He steers to find the shore from which we came,
> Fearless of in what coil he might be caught
>   On seas that have no name.
>
> Into the night he sails; and after night
>   There is a dawning, though there be no sun;
> Wherefore, with nothing but himself in sight,
>   Unsighted, he sails on.
>
> At last there is a lifting of the cloud
>   Between the flood before him and the sky;
> And then—though he may curse the Power aloud
>   That has no power to die—
>
> He steers himself away from what is haunted
>   By the old ghost of what has been before,—
> Abandoning, as always, and undaunted,
>   One fog-walled island more.   [472-473]

Though he refers specifically to science here, what Robinson says applies also to poetry and the poet: any attempt to discover the land from which we came turns up merely "one fog-walled island more." The poet can know only the passing phenomenon; never can he know life's origins and destiny.

By the time he wrote the letter to Will Durant previously quoted, Robinson had dropped every possible intellectual prop that could lend support to his commitment to poetry. There he claimed no more for it than that it was a personal light, capable of sustaining him against nothingness but not necessarily able to save anyone else. Certainly it could not save the world from its inexorable ongoing process. Nor does he make any larger claims for it in his later poems. Captain Craig's wondering leads, finally, from the identification of Christ and Buddha as poets to the cautious claim that

> Though he fail, or die,
> The poet somehow has the best of us;
> He has a gauge for us that we have not.   [1388]

Concerned with spirit, the inner man, the poet articulates man's best self, and in doing that he provides us with a moral measuring tape with which to know ourselves for what we are. Poetry is a moment of clarity in our self-knowledge as we pass through time, not the world's savior. Originally Robinson felt poetry could speak truth that was valid for all men, but later all he could claim for it was that it spoke the truth for one man— himself. In living through his vocation, he discovered that the poet, instead of being endowed with charismatic powers, instead of having a privileged point of reference or a special source of higher knowledge, was, like all men, inescapably engaged in life.

Poetry could remain Robinson's light while still suffering such diminishment because, instead of despairing when he could not objectively interpret life, he shifted his perspective somewhat and adopted another notion of truth—this time in the sense of realization of inner being or potential. Although in the early poem "Dear Friends," as already noted, he spoke of poems as "good glasses to read the spirit through" (84) as though he were a biologist with the soul a specimen for him to examine, by the time of "Captain Craig" (1898) he spoke of "the truth / to which we all are tending" (152)—which is somewhat ambiguous, since truth here could be either an inher-

33

ent inclination or an objective goal. In *Roman Bartholow* (1923) the ambiguity was dispelled in the lines,

> The seed of truth
> Is rooted in you, and the fruit is yours
> For you to eat alone.   [825]

When truth is inherent in the knower, man must turn his attention inward to perceive it. The mind must become passive and patiently wait for the light which comes not from the world through the senses, but by emanating from the subject. Forced to the wall at the dead end of the materialistic dualism he inherited, Robinson eluded the destructive hostility between the mind and the soul with which he had begun his poetic career by having the mind abandon its observer status. No longer aloof, detached, or aggressive, it submitted to its subject, listening instead of talking, serving instead of dominating.

At this point, the problem of truth becomes the problem of belief. The seed of truth can produce fruit only if the seed germinates, and, the mind being sterile, only belief can nourish it. With the estrangement of mind from soul, not one belief, but belief itself comes into question, as it did for William James and John Jay Chapman, thinkers pondering the basic issues while Robinson wrote about those issues in his poetry. Chapman wrote, in regard to James's "The Will to Believe," "But why all this pother—what difference does it make whether a man believes or not? Why is this question important enough to be discussed? . . . I had supposed that the idea of that note—the supposed connection between belief and conduct—was one of the busted ideas of the world, like astrology, or the divining rod?" To which James replied, "I am sorry for your paragraph about the supposed connection between belief and conduct. It is by no means busted; on the contrary, it is one of the most tremendous forces in the world." [9] At a time when belief itself was in doubt, James devoted himself, in this letter and in his philosophy, to vindicating it as a power. But as Ralph Barton Perry noted of James, "He was not credulous, but *suffered from incredulity*. He was deeply concerned with the need of belief

34

and with the right to believe, but made no considerable use of that right." [10]

The problem of belief, as James viewed it, and Robinson poetically articulated it, was more than a matter of making up one's mind about practical or ultimate issues. It was a question of the fundamental freedom to exercise vital powers toward an authentic life. The right to believe deeply concerned Robinson because in that right lay the means of releasing the deeper impulses of the spirit. James demanded, in "The Sentiment of Rationality," that philosophy "must define the future *congruously with our spontaneous* powers." [11] And throughout his philosophy he argued against materialism, determinism, and intellectualism—all rationalistic, closed views of the world that denied man's spirit freedom and scope—and for pluralism, pragmatism, and mysticism, which allowed the free play of man's deepest, most varied impulses. Robinson put his poetry in service to the same ends; it, too, was devoted to defining life congruently with man's spontaneous powers and derived its strength for that task from an open universe. Both writers were insisting upon not doctrine but belief in man, for only if he can believe in himself can man genuinely and fully be himself, can he know his truth, can he act, can the tremendous force of belief be exercised for good.

For Robinson as well as for James, then, the problem of truth was ultimately the problem of being able to free the soul from the world's prevailing darkness through belief.[12] He said as much at the end of "The Man Against the Sky":

> If after all we have lived and thought,
> All comes to Nought,—
> If there be nothing after Now,
> And if we be nothing anyhow,
> And we know that,—why live?
> 'Twere sure but weaklings' vain distress
> To suffer dungeons where so many doors
> Will open on the cold eternal shores
> That look sheer down
> To the dark tideless floods of Nothingness
> Where all who know may drown.   [68-69]

And both men were following in the footsteps of Emerson, who wrote, in "Experience," "in accepting the leading of the sentiments, it is not what we believe concerning the immortality of the soul or the like, but the universal impulse to believe, that is the material circumstance and principal fact in the history of the globe." [13] Belief is the very energy that propels and sustains life. Robinson explicitly expresses his agreement with Emerson in *Matthias at the Door*, where he has Timberlake, the wise man in the poem, say, "There is not a man who breathes and believes nothing" (1129). Without belief life is empty and futile, but

> If we believe enough
> In something—none shall tell another what—
> That's ours to do, we are glad to be alive,
> As Malory was, to do it.   [1012-1013]

Since life, at least conscious, human life, is purposive, since man must be able to affirm, explain, and give direction to his needs—breathing and believing are inherently necessary to one another. In a sense belief releases the breath. Uninhibited by doubt, the spirit lets itself go.

Robinson said in the lines quoted from *Roman Bartholow* that the truth within a man has to be eaten alone. The letter to Will Durant stated that a man can follow only his own light (significantly not capitalized); he cannot generalize from himself to mankind or the universe. Since every man's truth lies in the ineffable center of himself, in the mysterious power and direction of his unique life, no two individuals can know the spiritual significance of things in the same way. Every man attains the truth to which he is tending alone, and being his particular self-truth, it is not "negotiable" (1136). While persisting in his search for Truth, Robinson became less doctrinaire and more subtle intellectually as his understanding of things increased. Once the messenger of the Light, poetry became the light illuminating his personal way. But to write poems was to believe in poetry, and it was also to discover the truth about life in and through poetry; it was to find, that is, the truth of poetry, which is also the Truth of the spirit. Once his quest was oriented in that direction, accuracy of reference or representation was exposed as a lower order of truth and replaced by the highest order, sincerity, or faithful adherence to inner necessity. Intellectual fortitude came to mean for him the courage to see oneself for what one actually is. In his final and most profound notion of it, then, Robinson regards truth as a way of living in which a man remains true to himself. Truth is not so much proper knowledge as it is living truly; in fact, truth is life made manifest, for to live affirmatively rather than negatively, the outer forms of one's life must conform to his inner being.

Though Robinson toned down his claims about poetry, he never abandoned his belief in it. He never felt, as so many modern poets have, that the possibility and justification of poetry had to be established. Once he cleared his own mind of materialism, then poetry, or the impulse behind it, was the one absolutely given, indubitable fact for him. What was questionable about it was its intellectual significance, and since intellectual interpretation per se was questionable, all that remained for him in the end was poetry. Since the materialistic disjunction between mind and soul placed the soul beyond the comprehension of the mind, Robinson had to get along without any reflective knowledge, even regarding the power of poetry, to support his commitment to his vocation. To believe in poetry meant, finally, not to espouse an aesthetic doctrine, but to act, to be a poet, on faith; it was to take the risks of his calling with no props or security outside his performance as an artist. Robinson's progress from materialism to its antithesis was not an isolated achievement. The philosophy he repudiated had also left its traditional paths to seek out new ways of relating the mind to its subject. Though an original poet, Robinson was not an original thinker; lacking a taste and talent for analysis, he could not, like Yeats, for instance, equip his work with a theoretical counterpart. The major philosophers were, however, hammering out a vocabulary to make sense of the reality they had in common with Robinson, and their originality as thinkers offers a background against which to understand what was involved in Robinson's belief in poetry as well as what he accomplished as a poet.

Alfred North Whitehead, probably more responsible than any man for our present notions of Western intellectual history and himself a member of Edwin Arlington Robinson's generation, said of the last decades of the nineteenth century,

Within the period of sixty or seventy years preceding the present time, the progressive civilization of the European races has undergone one of the most profound changes in human history. The whole world has been affected; but the origination of the revolution is seated in the races of Western Europe and Northern America. It is a change of point of view. Scientific thought had developed with a uniform trend for four centuries, namely, throughout the sixteenth, seventeenth, eighteenth, and nineteenth centuries. In the seventeenth century, Galileo, Descartes, Newton, and Leibniz elaborated a set of concepts, mathematical and physical, within which the whole movement was confined. The culmination may be placed in the decade from 1870 to 1880. At that time Helmholtz, Pasteur, Darwin, and Clerk-Maxwell were developing their discoveries. It was a triumph which produced the death of a period. The change affects every department of thought.[14]

In Whitehead's large perspective, this period was in the throes of thorough intellectual re-examination and reconstruction, a genuine revolution in thought in which conceptions of man and the universe, and of the relation between them, were radically revised. More than a palace insurrection amounting to a change of kings while maintaining the old order, the revolution, as A. O. Lovejoy noted, was a battle of the twentieth century against the seventeenth over the fundamental principles on which the kingdom of knowledge was to stand.[15] It is thus quite appropriate to speak of these decades as a period of revolt—as a "revolt against dualism" or a "revolt against formalism" [16]—for it was truly a period of death and rebirth, a terminating and initiating stage out of which came the modern cosmology and mind.

A narrower focus than Whitehead's on this revolution, one that concentrates on man in society, is provided by H. Stuart Hughes, who wrote,

the axis of social thought was displaced from the apparent and objectively verifiable to the only partially conscious area of unexplained motivation. . . . It was no longer what actually existed that seemed most important: it was what men thought existed. . . . Since it had apparently been proved impossible to arrive at any sure knowledge of human behavior—if one must rely on flashes of subjective intuition and on the creation of convenient fictions—then the mind had indeed been freed from the bonds of positivist method: it was at liberty to speculate, to imagine, to create.[17]

In discussing European social thought, Hughes uses "consciousness" as his key term to characterize the central reality and value of the new thought. That term—or the concept it represents—does bring into focus the changes that occurred in philosophy, aesthetics, political thought, history, art, etc., in Europe. With it Bergson, Whitehead, Unamuno, Croce, to mention only philosophers, are readily linked together in the development of doctrines designed to articulate the emerging "feeling toward life," to use Unamuno's phrase. They all sensed, as Croce put it, that

We no longer believe like the Greeks, in happiness of life on earth; we no longer believe like the Christians, in happiness in an other-worldly life; we no longer believe, like the optimistic philosopher of the last century, in a happy future for the human race. . . . What we have alone retained is consciousness of ourselves, and the need to make that consciousness ever clearer and more evident, a need for whose satisfaction we turn to science and art.[18]

Sometimes employing the term informally, as Croce does here, but more often employing it (or a synonymous one) as a formal metaphysical category, these philosophers directed their thought toward determining the nature of the universe and life in a world which left man nothing but his consciousness.

Unfortunately "consciousness" does not serve quite so well as a term for characterizing the central reality and value in American thought. Although William James used it in the phrase "stream of consciousness" and it was fairly common in both philosophical and psychological parlance, the term lacked metaphysical status and so was not formally used to designate ultimate reality. This happened probably because James himself disqualified it for such use in his essay "Does 'Consciousness'

Exist?" where he argued, in A. O. Lovejoy's technical way of putting it, that " 'Consciousness as a kind of impalpable inner flowing,' a 'bare *Bewusstheit* or *Bewusstsein uberhaupt,*' evaporates to the 'state of pure diaphaneity'; it is, in short, not introspectively discoverable, and therefore does not exist." [19] James's argument is important—and was influential—not because it is his or true but because it reflects the differences in European and American habits of mind. While both European and American thinkers were investigating consciousness, the Europeans assumed that it existed as an a priori entity and that to understand reality it was therefore first necessary to understand consciousness. Giving the knower precedence over the known, they favored classical realism, which postulates the reality of universals and allows them to dominate the knowing process. Correspondingly, Russell, Whitehead, and Santayana, all scions of the European intellectual tradition, developed Platonistic doctrines. The American, on the other hand, assumed that consciousness resulted from the dramatic encounter of man with the world, from the pressure of outer events upon human sensibility. He therefore preferred naive realism, which gives epistemological equality to the external physical world, and favored voluntaristic philosophies such as pragmatism and instrumentalism that make the so-called universals relative to action. Thus Europeans and Americans tended to interpret consciousness in two different ways, the former understanding it to be an independent realm of mental entities, the latter taking its content to be replicas, or mirror images, referring to the things of nature; while the Europeans regarded it as "an indubitable datum" [20] given before and independent of experience, the American saw it as a consequence of and guide to action. It is the difference John Dewey had in mind when criticizing "ethereal things," or the traditional schism between intellect and body, in the statement,

The senses are the organs through which the live creature participates directly in the on-goings of the world about him. In this participation the varied wonder and splendor of the world are made actual for him in the qualities he experiences. The material cannot

40

be opposed to action, for motor apparatus and "will" itself are the means by which this participation is carried on and directed. It cannot be opposed to "intellect," for mind is the means by which meanings and values are extracted, retained, and put to further service in the intercourse of the live creature with his environment.[21]

No term that I know of had the kind of status in America that Hughes attributes to "consciousness" in Europe. However, William James, thinking about the same problems as the Europeans, did have a term roughly commensurate to the one he disqualified. That term is "radical empiricism." Because radical empiricism was James's special doctrine, it would be inaccurate to claim that it played a central role in the critical review that took place in America. Yet James's term, if taken as loosely representative of a climate of thought, does clarify the main thrust of the new thought in America at this time. In fact, James, aware that philosophy was "on the eve of a considerable rearrangement," wrote that "many minds are, in point of fact, now turning in a direction that points toward radical empiricism," [22] and thereby offered the term for such use.

Crucial to James's doctrine, and to the new sense of reality it represents, was a plain and thorough commitment to empiricism; "I am . . . a complete empiricist as far as my theory of human knowledge goes," [23] he once remarked. Little attention, however, was given by well-known American philosophers to empiricism as a formal philosophical position, and many of them, unsympathetic with British empiricism, deliberately avoided the term because of the traditional associations attached to it. Though he was as opposed as any of them to British empiricism, James did not avoid the word; he simply used it in a broader sense. He accepted the principle that all knowledge originates in the senses but denied that a reductive analysis of experience into atomistic sense impressions produced definitive knowledge of reality; his empiricism acknowledged a more complex testimony by the senses and entailed surrendering "the doctrine of objective certitude." It required that we "go on experiencing and thinking over our experience, for only thus can our opinions grow more true." [24] For James, reflective

41

thought does not stand outside experience as a looker-on and aloof recorder but participates in it. Bounded by experience, whose limits extend far beyond its own, reflective thought can never grasp the absolute, can never metaphysically encompass and exhaust the final truth; it sees the world not in its entirety but piecemeal, in accordance with a vantage point in space and time. For this reason James makes sentiment the arbiter of rationality, sometimes speaks of thoughts as feelings in his psychology, and always insists that thought becomes meaningless when divorced from living and regarded as an end in itself. Clearly, James's empiricism as a theory of human knowledge, like all forms of empiricism, gives the senses priority over reflective thought; but his is radical, and distinguished from the British variety, because it is based upon a concept of experience in which what the senses report to the intellect extends beyond the customary limits.

A clue to his concept is provided by Ralph Barton Perry in a statement he made about some of James's papers:

The manila envelope contained a manuscript on "A World of Pure Experience," and headed "Chapter I." The book of which this was to form the first chapter was to be called "Radical Empiricism"—signifying the "refusal to go beyond concrete experience," and the "insistence that conjunctive and disjunctive relations are, when experienced, equally real." [25]

In these notes James qualified "experience" with "pure" and "concrete," and in "Does 'Consciousness' Exist?" he defined experience as "the instant field of the present." [26] Then he described the attitude that must be taken toward that experience, and thereby defined radical empiricism as a method, by saying,

To be radical, an empiricism must neither admit into its constructions any element that is not directly experienced, nor exclude from them any element that is directly experienced. For such a philosophy, *the relations that connect experiences must themselves be experienced relations,* and any kind of relation experienced must be accounted as "real" as anything else in the system.[27]

British empiricists "weren't empirical enough" [28] for James; he assumed a complete or radical empiricism in which all of the senses, the internal as well as the external—or the entire content of consciousness—provide the data to be taken into account in explaining the nature of things, the external world as well as man's inner being. A. O. Lovejoy more formally stated this position when he summarized the basic argument proffered by the first phase of the revolt against dualism, for which James was a spokesman. "Since," Lovejoy wrote,

indirect or representative knowledge was assumed to be inconceivable, it must be held that the immediate content of an experience is always identical with the reality cognized in that experience. . . . Thus everything which is ever "before the mind" at all must be regarded as "objective." We must, it was proclaimed by the authors of the celebrated revolutionary manifesto, return to a metaphysical state of nature, to that "naive or natural realism" which "makes no distinction between seeming and being," but believes that "things *are* just what they seem." [29]

This epistemological principle, "starting from the immediate facts of our psychological experience, as surely an empiricist should begin," [30] though stated here so as to apply only to nature, actually opens the door to many other seemingly unnatural matters—to such things as belief, options or values, and religious experience. It allows James to investigate the varieties of religious experience rather than religious truths and to experiment with abnormal psychological states induced by drugs. These are or produce contents of consciousness as much "before the mind" as natural objects.

The position to which experience in Robinson's formative years reflectively leads,[31] then, is a new sense of the content and authority of experience in which the prereflective has priority over the conceptual, and conjunctive relations are as much given in experience as disjunctive relations. Emerson's call for Americans to enjoy an original relation with the universe and to return to the essential man is transformed by James into encouragement to return to and enjoy, or base our knowledge upon, pristine experience.

James's empiricism is to be distinguished not only from the British variety but also from what can be called scientific empiricism, which developed parallel to his but differs in granting a portfolio to only one of the senses—vision—and limits its purview to natural objects. Whereas British empiricism, initially an epistemology, is predominantly a doctrine about the way man knows, scientific empiricism, in James's time linked with materialism and scientism, is a doctrine about what can be known, a metaphysics defining reality. Typically represented by logical positivism and behaviorism, scientific empiricism is antimetaphysical (towards metaphysics other than its own) and antihumanistic. From its point of view speculative philosophical generalizations and matters of the heart or spirit are nonsense, not entities before the mind but emanations of ego-centered desires that obscure the tough reality of objects. This form of empiricism fastens its attention on the "thereness" of the external world of objects for the purpose of description, dissection, measurement, and causal analysis. James's empiricism is also methodologically objective, but it does not so thoroughly discipline the intellect in subservience to "facts." Its subject is pure and concrete experience, which means that man's intellect and emotions contribute directly to what is known. James turns empiricism upon experience in order to know the content and structure of consciousness, which is equated with the content and structure of the world. Because consciousness and the world are equated, James's empiricism tolerates metaphysics; in fact, as James intended eventually to use the term, radical empiricism is a name for a metaphysical doctrine, though he never completely formulated it.

At the same time that it acknowledges the limits of reason in subordinating reason to feeling, radical empiricism also opens new frontiers for reflective thought and encourages it to explore and chart that territory. Thus the new thought articulates a sense of life in which the traditional antinomies of subject and object are avoided by putting the mind back into nature.

The life of the mind for the philosopher as well as the poet began diseased with a sort of intellectual schizophrenia. Concentration on the disjunctive aspects of experience over several centuries had estranged the mind from reality; the Faustian drive for knowledge ended, ironically, in an impotent reason. To remedy the mind's malady, it was necessary to switch its allegiance to the conjunctive aspects in experience. And to do that, it was unavoidable that reason be employed to destroy rationalism, its own nature generalized as primordial reality. But as soon as that suicidal course was set out upon, the philosopher was trapped in a contradiction which made him vulnerable to a standard attack such as Henri Bergson long endured. How could he use reason to disqualify itself and therefore philosophy and still ask that his philosophy be taken seriously? Logical consistency required that he either regard reason, and the disjunctive aspects of experience, as final truth, or he must be silent. Or he could abandon logical consistency and turn to aesthetic modes for the key to truth, humbling himself, reason, and philosophy before the throne of art. This, of course, is what he did, and since James wrote, philosophers and theologians have more and more relied upon art as a replacement for revelation, a priori principles, and natural law in their reflections on the nature of things worldly and divine.

Both philosopher and poet shared a common intellectual heritage, and both, desiring a unitive thought and art, pushed the mind toward a relation with the world and the soul conducive to unity, life, and action. In bringing the individuated and individuating faculty into a viable connection with the ground from which it emerged, however, the philosopher was at a distinct disadvantage. Reflective thought is inherently analytical, so it cannot but attend to and exalt the disjunctive aspects of experience. The imagination, on the other hand, naturally favors the conjunctive aspects; what it does first and best is to synthesize. Though he wrote an intellectual poetry, Robinson by his vocation was inside what the philosopher was forever excluded from. He could speak with a directness and authority forever denied the man of reason. Whereas the philosopher had to live with a disabling doubt about his own powers, the poet could believe with unquenchable conviction in his, as Robinson did. In the dark and awful chaos of the old order's night, Robinson was advantageously endowed to assist in the demise of rationalism, and the delivery of the new order. His poetry contained the conjunctive power to heal his divided being and perhaps that of his culture as well.

The shadowed word

They have science; but in science there
is nothing but what is the object of
sense. The spiritual world, the higher
part of man's being, is rejected altogether, dismissed with a sort of triumph,
even with hatred.

Dostoievski

Despite Robinson's unwavering belief, all was not right
with poetry; that, I think, is apparent now. Probably the major
challenge to his belief, certainly to his uttering truth in poetic
form, was language, his artistic medium. When Robinson found
the mind divorced from the soul, he also was confronted by a
language divorced from reality, and so disqualified as a direct
spokesman for things as they actually are. To succeed in his
aspiration, Robinson, as a consequence, had to find a substitute
for words, a vehicle capable of bearing his imagination's utter-
ances about the truth of the spirit.

In the following passages, his fullest poetic statements on
the subject, Robinson defines the relation of language to reality
as he understood it. The first is from "The Man Against the
Sky" (1915), where the speaker says, as part of his concluding
speculations on man's knowledge of his own nature and destiny:

> Shall we, because Eternity records
> Too vast an answer for the time-born words
> We spell, whereof so many are dead that once

47

In our capricious lexicons
Were so alive and final, hear no more
The Word itself, the living word
That none alive has ever heard
Or ever spelt . . . [68]

The second is from *Matthias at the Door* (1931), where
Garth, as a voice from the dead attempting to dissuade Matthias
from committing suicide, says, in the course of his argument
that life must be accepted without final knowledge of its meaning:

"Language, Matthias,
With a few finite and unfinished words
That are the chips of brief experience,
You restless and precipitate world-infants
Would build a skiff to circumnavigate
Infinity, and would find it, if you could,
No more sufficient or more commodious
Or comprehensive in its means and habit
Than a confused, confined phenomenon
Prisoned within a skull, with knowledge in it.
There's not much knowledge in it, and less wisdom."
[1151]

Although the first passage affirms the Word and the second
negates words, both emphatically repudiate the assumption that
language can truly represent reality.

The key to Robinson's sense of spirit, and therefore to his
subject, lies in "the Word" and "infinity." The spiritual was not
to be found everywhere. It was decidedly not to be found in
nature, for instance. For Emerson, nature spoke to man, edu-
cating his soul in matters spiritual, beaming or reflecting a
powerful, deeply penetrating light into the depths of his being.
Because he could know himself through his identity with nature, man's relation and response to it was an essential subject
for Emerson, and the Transcendentalists in general. Through
solitude in nature the soul could slough off its social skin and
expand to a vastness correspondent to the scenic grandeur before it, thereby obtaining a renewed sense of its true being and
power. For Robinson this was not so. "You won't find much in
the way of natural description," he said of his poetry; "There is

very little tinkling water, and there is not a red-bellied Robin in the whole collection. When it comes to 'nightingales and roses' I am not 'in it' nor have I the smallest desire to be." [1] The light that shone so brilliantly in nature for Emerson and became a momentary, fleeting gleam in spring for Emily Dickinson [2] had been completely put out by materialism for Robinson.

His indifference to nature, especially as it was regarded by the Transcendentalists and Romantics, obviously amounted to more than a change in taste; it was a radically altered conception of the world man inhabits. "I'm afraid, on the whole," he wrote on this point, "that there isn't much comfort in nature as a visible evidence of God's visible love. It appears to be a shambles and a torture-chamber from the insects up—or should we say down?" [3] Mechanism and materialism, demanding an absolute separation between man and nature, with the consequence that man is forced to regard himself as "a sort of outside passenger travelling across a fundamentally alien environment," [4] killed nature. Whenever nature does occur in Robinson's poetry, it is bleak and cold, or associated with the darker states of mind such as hopelessness, or used to emphasize man's alienation from his environment; in "Luke Havergal" Luke is told not to "think to riddle the dead words" the fallen leaves say, "nor any more to feel them as they fall." Nature's death can tell man nothing significant about his own.

When nature became inhospitable to spirit for Robinson, he recognized that man, if he stands upright at all, stands alone; he is the only instance of spirit and therefore the only evidence of its nature and destiny. When self-knowledge cannot come through communication with nature, man must turn inward or to his kind—to introspection or to what is "between man and man." With nature dead, man must open himself to man, to his spiritual being mirrored in his own reflection or the fate of others. For this reason Robinson's immediate subject is man. Nowhere does he announce this fact in so many words, yet there can be no doubt about it, his entire poetic work being cogent testimony of it. Judging from his titles alone—for example, "Luke Havergal," "Eben Flood," "Captain Craig," "Merlin,"

"King Jasper"—it is clear that individual man is the essential spiritual phenomenon for him. But there is other evidence also. There is, for instance, his remark on Kipling's animal stories, "My taste in this direction corresponds with my indifference to the doings of trained animals. I prefer men and women who live, breathe, fight, make love, or go to the devil after the manner of human beings. Art is only valuable to me when it reflects humanity or at least human emotions." [5] There are the lines in "Zola":

> Never until we conquer the uncouth
> Connivings of our shamed indifference
> (We call it Christian faith) are we to scan
> The racked and shrieking hideousness of Truth
> To find, in hate's polluted self-defense
> Throbbing, the pulse, the divine heart of man.   [85]

And on repeated occasions in his letters when judging a work of literature or another man, he is especially concerned about the quality of humanity. "I am getting more and more convinced," he once remarked, "that Daudet is the greatest artist in fiction now living—and his art never crowds out his humanity." [6] Humanity, human emotions, the divine heart of man—these terms refer to and identify the distinctive location of the spiritual reality that Robinson sought to know. It is this reality, for example, that the speakers of "Flammonde" and "The Man Against the Sky" seek so strenuously to understand.

Only through knowledge of the spiritual significance of things can man know himself, and conversely, only through self-knowledge can he know the spiritual significance of things. Thus, to complete his quest for truth Robinson had to have access to the inner being of man. However, he found man's inner being highly elusive. "Nothing is there more marvelous than man," [7] he translated a line in Sophocles' *Antigone*, and he liked it so much that he used it in "Captain Craig." Truly man is marvelous, for he is a spiritual being, the only one in this world, but being that he is also unfathomable. He is as vast and as deep as the infinite and eternal spiritual reality that is the source of his being. Of a very early poem, "The Night Before," one of the title pieces of *The Torrent and the Night Before,* his first volume, Robinson said, "The main purpose of the thing is to show that men and women are individuals." [8] Included in the volume were such poems as "John Evereldown," "Eben Flood," "Miniver Cheevy," "Luke Havergal," and "Richard Cory"—all poems with individuals, most of them quite eccentric ones, as their subjects. In showing that men and women were individuals Robinson not only placed them in conflict with their society but assumed that a man's innermost self was beyond the reach of intellectual apprehension.

For if each person is defined by his individuality, his identity lies in what he himself is, not in any external relation. Each person is autonomous and cannot be subsumed under general principles or laws. "There is more in every person's soul than we think," Robinson said in his most general comment on this matter. "Even the happy mortals we term ordinary or commonplace act their own mental tragedies and live a far deeper and wider life than we are inclined to believe possible in the light of our own prejudices." [9] About a dead friend, whom others were judging, he said, "A suicide signifies discouragement or despair either of which is, or should be, too far beyond the scope of our piddling human censure to require of our ignorance anything less than silence." [10] And even when he would seem most tempted to speak out against a man who was his antithesis in temperament, taste, and morality, he honored the individual's inviolability. "As for my Lord Byron," he once wrote, "I don't know what to say, considering life as the hopelessly mixed up and imperfect mess that it is. . . . If one knew all the circumstances (which we never do), perhaps there might be found at least a passive or scratchy defense of his action, or lack of it." [11] Peculiar as it may seem, Robinson granted the same unencroachable, ultimate privacy to his fictional characters. "Richard Cory" is perhaps the best-known example of his respect for the inaccessible recesses of man's inner being, but his most explicit acknowledgment of it is his remark on "Doctor of

51

Billiards." It "pictures a man," he said, "who seems to be throwing away a life which, for some reason known only to himself, is no longer worth living." [12]

Individual man turns out to be as impossible to comprehend as the objective meaning of life, for not the essence but only the outer form—the speech, gestures, acts, etc.—of the individual is knowable. Yet Robinson's inability to satisfy his hunger for truth results as much from an attitude toward language as it does from a conception of reality. Implied in the passages quoted from "The Man Against the Sky" and *Matthias at the Door,* Robinson's attitude toward language, is, in a word, that of nominalism. Flax, a character in *Amaranth,* explicitly adopts this view when he says,

> There is no God
> For me to fear, or none that I may find,
> Or feel, except a living one within me,
> Who tells me clearly, when I question him,
> That he is there. There is no name for him,
> For names are only words. There was a time
> When I thought words were life.   [1387]

Flax is unquestionably speaking for Robinson here. Repeatedly in his poetry Robinson comments on the incommensurability of language and reality, and in a letter, where this conviction occurs as a personal rather than a poetic utterance, he comments, "Nothing of an infinite nature can be proven or disproven in finite terms—meaning words." [13] Words are not life, only labels for what appears to be, and thus they open no doors to the intangible, spiritual reality within man. Between the finite and infinite, between appearance and reality, between words and the Word, lies an impenetrable shadow.

Nominalism is usually linked with the skepticism of British empiricism and such recent schools of philosophy as logical positivism and general semantics, all of which maintain that because words are only names man cannot know reality, only its ephemeral appearances, if even that. But nominalism, it must be remembered, was also professed by Duns Scotus, a devout Roman Catholic priest for whom the limitations of language are not the limitations of human knowledge. Robinson's nominalism is of the Duns Scotus variety: although he denies the efficacy of language in the quest to know ultimate reality, he does not abandon the assumption that the Word exists and is knowable. Flax, for instance, despite his disbelief in words, finds that the Word is there, living within him, when he seeks it in the right manner. In probably his best-known remark—certainly his most vivid one—on the relation of language to reality, Robinson said, "The world is not a 'prison house,' but a kind of kindergarten, where millions of bewildered infants are trying to spell God with the wrong blocks." [14] Though language failed Robinson in his quest for the Word, the search continued; Robinson persevered in his effort to comprehend that Something of an infinite nature existing beyond the pales of language. Despite the limitations of language, the Word remained for Robinson an ineluctable reality that could somehow, to some degree, be known, and his primary problem as a craftsman was to find the right blocks with which to spell it.

It is a curious phenomenon indeed when a poet finds it necessary to distrust and even repudiate his medium, when he finds it necessary to regard as the "wrong blocks" the very material he must employ to build his towers of significance. Robinson persisted in his aspiration to "spell" reality, but more and more realized that something was wrong with language. In the passage previously quoted from "The Man Against the Sky," he asserts that because they are spiritually dead, words which once were alive and final no longer are capable of recording eternity or truth. The language Robinson had at his disposal for writing poetry, though he could not have described it this way, was the language of British and scientific empiricism, a strictly denotative language limited to the one function of reference, of pointing to discrete natural objects or events. This language is based on an assumption that abstractions of a high degree are the primary ingredients of experience. Once these abstractions, sifted out of the experience continuum by a conceptual net, are regarded as reality, then the language which refers to them becomes stripped of its moral and religious di-

mensions of meaning. When this happens, poetry no longer
exists in the objective world and the language which refers to it
is of little or no use for aesthetic purposes.

F. W. Bateson, in his fine study *English Poetry and the
English Language,*[15] has shown specifically how this denudation
of language was significant in nineteenth-century English poetry. One point he makes, of special relevance here, is that since
Wordsworth's Preface to the *Lyrical Ballads,* the language of
prose has also been the language of poetry. Language in the
nineteenth century had neither the natural "poetic" quality it
did for the Elizabethans nor the special vocabulary of poetic
diction associated with a special poetic realm, such as the neo-
classical poets relied upon. For the writer there was simply the
language of prose, and whether used for scientific or general
essays or for fiction, this was the language of realism—the
language of scientific materialism, British empiricism, and the
British novel that Francis Bacon and Thomas Hobbes defined
as appropriate for the scientific view of the world and that
emerged with science and the art that flourished alongside it,
namely prose fiction. In the nineteenth century, when science
completed its conquest of the Western mind and imagination, it
became *the* language. Commenting on this fact, W. B. Yeats
remarked about William Morris, "His age offered him a speech
exhausted from abstraction,"[16] and once observed of himself,
". . . I began to pray that my imagination might somehow be
rescued from abstraction."[17] All his efforts as artist and thinker,
his style as well as his ideas on symbolism and emotion, were
clearly intended to make that rescue possible. A contemporary
of Yeats, Robinson, too, as already noted, was bothered by abstraction, and to carry through his poetic task, he had to rescue
his imagination from its debilitating effects. Inescapably, his
attempt to get rid of materialism was simultaneously an attempt
to free himself from the "dead" language of realism.

The most obvious effect of materialism on Robinson's medium, then, was to strip away from language those dimensions
of meanings by which poetry is nourished. Paradoxical as it

may seem, however, Robinson was himself a realist in aesthetics, and not only early in his career when he is obviously so, but at the end of it as well. In fact, it was because he accepted the aesthetics of realism that language proved so hostile to his purposes, for that aesthetics assumes a subject-object dualism in which meaning is regarded as a one-to-one relation between concept or image and reality. Postulating a separation between the word and its referent, realism automatically makes problematic the relation of thought, language, and art to reality.

That realism shaped Robinson's attitudes early in his career is unquestionable. As a beginning writer he gave a great deal of time to fiction and even planned and wrote a volume of apparently realistic short stories which he intended to publish. Subsequently he changed his mind and destroyed them, but in the meantime he read widely among the British and American realists; spoke highly of Kipling, Thackeray, Hardy, Henry James, and Bret Harte, among others; read the realist critics in the current periodicals; and referred to his own work as well as that of others in such a way as to leave no doubt that "reality" was his primary concern as thinker and artist. He was familiar, for instance, with the attitude of his friend Thomas Sergeant Perry, of whom he said, "Novels mostly wearied him. 'If they are true to life,' he would say, 'they are only depressing. If they are not true to life, they are only silly.' . . . He liked best the things he could see and feel and get hold of." [18] Robinson's artistic instincts would not allow him to dismiss a literary genre so readily himself, but he employed substantially the same argument when he said, in regard to the *Rubaiyat* of Omar Khayyam, "A little bit of reality applied would knock these old poets into a cocked hat." [19] Like Perry, he, too, used reality as a test. "I have just read Hamlin Garland's little obstetrical story in the Chap-Book," he wrote in a letter, "and . . . I rather like it. It is strong and true to life, according to my notions. . . . I cannot say that I agree with Mr. Garland's idea of realism—what it should be, but the story is good. . . ." [20] Robinson was more than just familiar with realism: he assumed that trueness to life, verisimilitude, attention to *Wirklichkeit,* is a valid criterion for literature, and he even had his own special idea of realism.

Now realism in its broadest sense—and this is true of philosophical as well as literary realism—assumes an ontological order beyond human consciousness, a world of substantial things or universal laws existing independently of a subject. When thinking correctly the mind adapts its thought to the world beyond it, taking its shape from an external source to which it conforms. There is a tendency in American literature studies to think of literary realism as those attitudes William Dean Howells spoke for and helped to establish as the basis of modern American fiction. But as Erich Auerbach has shown in *Mimesis*,[21] literary realism is a long-standing tradition in Western thought, based on the conception of art as representing the objective order of time and space that man inhabits as a creature of this world. Viewed in this context Howells' realism is but one species of the genus, comparable, say, to Homeric realism, Old Testament realism, or Rabelaisian realism. Howells' realism rests upon a specific conception of the world, one which, following the lead of materialistic-mechanistic science, assumes that a permanent, objective, universal truth—a moral law—informs the universe and is available as objective knowledge to all men. Such a conception, though appropriate for most of Howells' work and that of his contemporaries, cannot validly be applied, for instance, to the work of Virginia Woolf or to Lawrence Durrell's *Alexandria Quartet,* for these writers work with a different idea of the ontological order that man inhabits. Whereas Howells worked within the old Newtonian cosmology, Woolf and Durrell work within the new Einsteinian one, obviously representing the natural world, but a different one from the one Howells represents, and their work differs accordingly in structure and style.

In Howells' realism, which might be called prosaic realism, everything, including man, is seen from a spectator's point of view and becomes an object, an entity separate from mind that is known empirically and conceptually. Robinson began as a

56

Howellsian realist; the natural world, including man, was there, had a certain character, and could be known in a certain way. In the course of his career, however, he changed his mind regarding man's relation to and knowledge of his world and himself. Much more philosophically inclined than Howells, with his socially oriented fiction, and as a poet ultimately opting for the inner life rather than the outer form, Robinson abandoned the inadequate attitudes deriving from materialism and emerged not an antirealist but a realist of a more profound kind. When Robinson disagreed with Hamlin Garland's idea of realism, he was probably rejecting Howells' with something in mind like Wallace Stevens' remark that "Realism is a corruption of reality." [22] At any rate, he sought to replace Howells' prosaic realism with poetic realism, a trueness to life that would not be a corruption of poetry's truth. Robinson learned by trial and error that realistic fiction, like science, confines itself to the world as it appears to be, viewing man either as a social creature whose "soul" is manifested in manners and morals or as a helpless victim to overwhelming natural forces that play on and about him. Significantly, no such animal as "realistic poetry" exists; poetry by nature favors a truth more exalted than that revealed by empirical vision.[23]

The course Robinson took to counteract the language and aesthetics of realism is most readily apparent in his reaction to objectivity, realism's most cherished value. Robinson acknowledged its value and was a self-professed objectivist. In endorsing Cestre's study of his poetry, for instance, he approved of Cestre's main thesis that his poetry is classical, and that his "Classic restraint is too strong . . . to allow him ever to depart from the strict principle of objectivity." [24] Moreover, a perceptive grammar school teacher's characterization of him as "a highly sensitive child, looking at the world objectively, for the most part, and quick to observe the humor in everything," [25] is supported by his remark, in 1894, that ". . . the majority of mankind interest me only as studies. They are to me 'a little queer,' like the Quaker's wife. . . . I do a considerable amount of observing . . . it opens one's eyes to the question of happiness and leads him to analyze that mysterious element in human nature from many points of view." [26] And whereas W. B. Yeats, an explicit subjectivist, could say, commenting on the malady of the modern world, "I am very sad, for comedy, objectivity, has displayed its growing power once more," [27] Robinson could say, of a planned trilogy, "It will be comical as the deuce, and, somewhat unlike 'Captain Craig,' almost wholly objective. . . . You will find the original ME as far away from the text as you find it now in little John Evereldown." [28]

The degree to which objectivity was a self-conscious phenomenon for Robinson is humorously apparent in a remark made by Thomas Sergeant Perry and quoted by Robinson in his introduction to Perry's letters. "An earnest medievalist who deplored the encroachments of time and change, especially the formation of republics [said], 'Perry, there are times when I yearn to be a subject.' 'What's the matter? [replied Perry.] Aren't you contented with being an object?' " [29] Evidence that objectivity wasn't a joking matter usually but a highly regarded antidote for vague sentiments and fuzzy writing is offered by his recommendation of it to Josephine Preston Peabody:

E. A. Robinson exhorting me to drop 'philosophizing' and twittering at infinities and to write about things objective. Want to, but how can I without being D—d pessimistic? . . . I wonder how many years it is that I've had to drown this quarterly rebellion. . . . It comes as inexorably as noon; and it's always the same, only worse—and its always as helpless as a Calvinistic hell. Positively the one sure fact of my objective world (and—ye terrestial gnats—what an ache in the nape of my weary little neck).[30]

She tried to see the world with Robinson's recommended objectivity, and succeeded, but she had no stomach for the tough, bleak, unfeminine self-denial it entailed. Objectivity was simply in the air Robinson breathed; it inevitably became engrained in his sense of the world and himself; and so it comes as no surprise that it permeates his poetry, and that what he said of Zola as a novelist is equally true of himself as a poet—that he was a "worker in the objective." [31]

And throughout his entire career, although he explored

many of the possibilities of form and feeling within the limits of that perspective, he never abandoned objectivity. One of the outstanding features of modern poetry has been its pronounced subjectivity, which is reflected in the widespread use of the first-person point of view and symbolism. This subjectivity is not to be equated, of course, with the subjectivity of Romantic poets, which is characterized by direct expression of sentiment, but it does make poetry the vehicle for direct human expression. For Robinson, however, subjectivity of all kinds is aesthetically and psychologically unpalatable. He commented on Yeats, who has been a major influence in modern poetry:

Mr. W. B. Yeats looks as if he might have the afflatus, and pretty badly, too. His picture is not what one has a right to look for in this nineteenth century, and I am too conservative to admire the taste that leads a man to make a "holy show" of himself.[32]

The kind of poetry that could be written in his time, as he saw it, excluded directly expressing sentiment or self.

Robinson's quarrel with Hamlin Garland, or the prose realists, was not intended to repudiate objectivity; it issued from his awareness that a certain kind of objectivity—naive objectivity, it might be called, which regards the objects of vision or intellectual concepts as reality—was inadequate for a poet. Despite all his concern with and praise for objectivity, he had to say, "Just as deliberate pathos in literature—that is, pathos for 'effect' alone—is almost always a mistake, so, I think, is objectivity . . . at the best unsatisfactory." [33] This unsatisfactoriness is inherent in the difference between poetry and prose. Essentially denotative, prose can commit itself to fact, but poetry is always song and so automatically proclaims the supremacy of inner power over outer circumstances. As a realist, Robinson, like Flax in *Amaranth,* turned his eyes away from external things inward to the Word living within him. Unconsciously following William James's lead, Robinson recognized that for art to be true to life, one had to accept consciousness or experience per se as empirical fact. Unamuno, a contemporary of these men, in reacting to the same circumstances, vigorously spoke for Robinson when he said, in *The Tragic Sense of Life,*

And what all the objectivists do not see, or rather do not wish to see, is that when a man affirms his "I," his personal consciousness, he affirms man, man concrete and real, affirms the true humanism—the humanism of man, not the things of man—and in affirming man he affirms consciousness. For the only consciousnes of which we have consciousness is that of man.

The world is for consciousness. Or rather this *for,* this notion of finality, the feeling rather than notion, this teleological feeling, is born only where there is consciousness. Consciousness and finality are fundamentally the same thing.

If the sun possessed consciousness it would think, no doubt, that it lived in order to give light to the worlds; but it would also and above all think that the worlds existed in order that it might give them light and enjoy itself in giving them light and so live. And it would think well.[34]

Like Unamuno, Robinson rejected naive objectivity—or scientific empiricism—because turned upon man or oneself it excluded the subject from the world, and the negation or alienation this entailed would have prohibited his studying man. This does not mean that Robinson abandoned objectivity as a point of view, but rather that he insisted, like William James, that certain aspects of human experience be admitted as a valid concern for thought or literature. He modified naive objectivity by redefining experience in the same way it was defined in radical empiricism. Robinson did in his poetry, for example, what William James did in *Varieties of Religious Experience,* where James sought to make a contribution to the science of religion by empirically analyzing what he himself refers to as the idealistic aspects of experience. This kind of objectivity, a familiar device in modern literature—as exemplified by the poetry of T. S. Eliot and the prose of Ernest Hemingway—sweeps away the accidental, egotistical elements of personality in order to bare the essential, universal self.

Because he scrupulously honored the limits of objectivity upon point of view at all times, his means of painting the inner world in an objective age [35] were achieved in a manner consistent with them. He has a reputation for being obscure, and critics have on occasion been inclined to make much of his obscurity as a defect in his poetry. But odd as it may seem, he claimed the obscurity was intentionally there. In a remark already cited on a sonnet titled "Supremacy," he said, "The verses in question must be taken as rather vague generalities: they will not bear, and I never intended them to bear, definite analysis." [36] And on another occasion, more generally, he said, "I have encountered so much rotten imbecility in the way of failure to get my meaning that I am beginning to wonder myself if it may not be vague. But I won't have it anything worse than obscure, which I meant it to be—to a certain extent." [37] He was naturally inclined to obscurity to begin with: "Habitually, in conversation," Elizabeth Bates observed, "he made oblique statements, or statements of implication, only. Because of a deep-seated caution and an equally deep reserve, he disliked being required to be explicit." [38] Perhaps in conversation obscurity was a protective strategy, but what could its point be in a poem? Why would he say of a poem he was working on that he had the problem "of keeping the idea of destiny ever present without saying much about it"? [39] One reason might be that he wanted to keep the poem from being confused with the idea, from being regarded as merely philosophy. But there is a deeper reason. He deliberately cultivated obscurity because the truth he sought to utter even in his early poetry, when ideas could be subjects of poems, could not be objectively stated; the words of realistic language being deficient, such truth had to be hinted at, suggested, presented indirectly or obliquely.

Correspondingly, as he became more sophisticated about truth, he became more intent upon, and more proficient at, cultivating obscurity. Like Howells, and in accordance with the interests of realism, he regarded his work in the early stage of his career as largely "an attempt to show the poetry of the commonplace." [40] Though his theory and practice were in some ways as incongruent as Wordsworth's in *Lyrical Ballads,* he sought, nevertheless, to make poetry out of, or to find poetry in, the real as he understood it at this time—things as they visually are. Consequently, his early poems at their best tended to be tight, succinct, sharp, concrete, lucid, vivid, exact. Poems like "Flammonde," "Richard Cory," "Eben Flood," though each in different ways, derive their power from concreteness, from clarity achieved through sharp observation. Instead of practice resulting in greater concreteness and vividness, which might seem the logical and customary course, he became progressively more obscure, until in the late long poems his narratives are so dimly motivated and tortuously plotted that it is a major task just to determine what happens in them. These poems are in no way devoted to the poetry of the commonplace, and as a consequence the language in them becomes relatively dissociated from things seen, actual speech, and concrete situations. Passionate, long-winded talk; general, abstract diction; relatively formal, "high-toned" syntax; circumlocution and rhetoric become in them the hallmarks of Robinson's style.

Evidence that he had not simply lost his poetic power in the long poems but was adapting his style to a profounder understanding of his subject is found in Robinson's statements about the nature of poetry. Of *Van Zorn,* which he called "more a poem than a play," he said, "The play is for the most part the working of character upon character, the plot being left, more or less, to reveal itself by inference." [41] A play, this remark implies, presents explicitly; a poem suggests, hints of things dimly felt. Communication between people in his poems is always by way of the tone of a remark or expression with the eyes, never just through language, and his characters' convictions are always based on feeling rather than clearly conceived ideas. Moreover, though Robinson never conceptualizes spiritual reality, almost every poem testifies to its existence by creating an aura or situation that suggests a hidden life beyond the explicit language of the poem. And in the light of his remark, "I suppose I always depended rather more on context than on vocabulary for my poetical effects," [42] what was true for his characters was also true for his poems.

He had by the time of this last remark learned that the poetry in a poem resides primarily in the form, the tone, the style, those intangible elements that encompass and permeate the specific words and hold them in suspension, thereby allowing poetry to tell us what cannot be said. This amounted to the discovery on his own, simultaneously with the psychologists and philosophers, of the now well-established fact that meaning resides primarily in the context. George Herbert Mead, who was almost exactly contemporary with Robinson, stated what Robinson learned, in *Mind, Self and Society,* when he noted, "We want to approach language not from the standpoint of inner meanings to be expressed, but in the larger context of co-operation in the group taking place by means of signals and gestures. Meaning appears within that process." [43] Through his labors as a poet on his recalcitrant medium, Robinson came to understand that objective language had no syncretistic powers, only analytic ones, and that consequently meaning did not reside in words themselves, the abstract counters of the mind, but in the situations in which they occur. Words, he realized, had to be shadowed to reveal the shadowed Word, as he referred to his subject in "L'Envoi." Obscurity, paradoxically, was a prerequisite of clarity.

In some ways cultivating obscurity was undoubtedly a mistake, since it weakened the vivid impact his poetry originally had and all poetry benefits by; yet as a blatant sign that Robinson had hit upon the equivalence of form and content, it establishes an early instance in America of what F. W. Bateson has called "the return to structure" in modern poetry.[44] He did not make this return in quite so experimental and dramatic a fashion as some subsequent poets have; nevertheless, he did make it. He was aware that poetry was statement without syntax and that therefore the poem as a whole—its overall form, not any statement within it—was the block for spelling the Word.

Making it as incisively and as early as he did, that return to structure placed him at the vital center in the emergence of twentieth-century poetry and is the key to his stature within its development. Beginning with the French symbolists, the modern poet has found language as much a hindrance as a help in his efforts to render reality aesthetically and has employed a wide variety of strategies, including extra-linguistic devices in many cases, to overcome its deficiencies. At times he has even argued that the poet should dispense with language altogether, though he has never quite succeeded in doing so in practice. Elizabeth Sewell, for example, says of Valéry, "he curses words in good round terms, calling them impure, incoherent, unreliable, trombones, parrots, idols, but they were none the less his only medium." [45] But whatever his strategies, the modern poet has almost always adopted the attitude that language cannot represent reality and so the heart of a poem has been located in its non-discursive aesthetic elements. Yeats, to cite an example at random, said:

. . . from this return to imagination, this understanding that the laws of art, which are the hidden laws of the world, can alone bind the imagination, would come a change of style, and one would cast out of serious poetry those energetic rhythms, as of a man running, which are the invention of the will with its eyes always on something to be done or undone; and we would seek out those wavering, meditative, organic rhythms, which are the embodiment of the imagination, that neither desires nor hates, because it has done with time, and only wishes to gaze upon some reality, some beauty; nor would it be any longer possible for anybody to deny the importance of form, in all its kinds, for although you can expound an opinion, or describe a thing when your words are not quite well chosen, you cannot give a body to something that moves beyond the senses, unless your words are as subtle, as complex, as full of mysterious life, as the body of a flower or of a woman. [46]

What Yeats says is also substantially true of Robinson and those poets who, unlike himself, were not convinced that the laws of art are necessarily the laws of a remote, divine reality. They, too, would agree that art must give body to something that moves beyond the senses, beyond language, though that something, they would perhaps maintain, is natural rather than supernatural.

Now, despite some expressed notions to the contrary, Robinson sought from the beginning of his career to tell the truth about the something that moves beyond the senses, and finding the words in objective language without subtlety, complexity, or mysterious life, he fell back upon aesthetic devices, mainly point of view and narrative structure, as a language for giving utterance to the truth he perceived. Others, those who have been more favorably judged in the last few decades, have relied more heavily on symbol and myth to accomplish this poetic end. Robinson, essentially a narrative poet, did no more, however, than to test briefly the experimental modes. A storyteller, he preferred instead to adapt the common features of the narrative art to his vision.

"Credo," from *The Children of the Night* (1897), is a poem from his first period, which extends through the *Town Down the River:*

> I cannot find my way: there is no star
> In all the shrouded heavens anywhere:
> And there is not a whisper in the air
> Of any living voice but one so far
> That I can hear it only as a bar
> Of lost, imperial music, played when fair
> And angel fingers wove, and unaware,
> Dead leaves to garlands where no roses are.
>
> No, there is not a glimmer, nor a call,
> For one that welcomes, welcomes when he fears,
> The black and awful chaos of the night;
> For through it all—above, beyond it all—
> I know the far-sent message of the years,
> I feel the coming glory of the Light.   [94]

Formally, the poem is a statement, the "I" simply relating its predicament—mainly, of course, by means of metaphor, a not-so-simple poetic device. Since it is addressed to no one in particular, it serves largely as self-expression and self-clarity, and as such is dangerously inclined toward maudlin self-pity or vain self-advertisement. But the statement is sufficiently objective to avoid that. The speaker keeps hold of himself, and appropriately, for his words issue from the mind, not his undoubtedly turbulent spiritual or emotional recesses. (The sonnet, incidentally, has all the right rationalistic qualities—a tightly formal stanzaic structure, meter, and rhyme scheme—to embody an utterance by the reflective mind.) In effect the mind or consciousness, the knowing faculty, testifies simultaneously to its need to understand and its inability to do so. The subject it focuses upon, try as it will, remains dim and remote. Through its observer-reflector point of view and an act which consists of making a pronouncement, "Credo" defines the mind's relation to its subject, if it makes much sense to speak of such an oblique and indirect connection as a relation. The truth about things is that the speaker's consciousness is so divorced from reality that only the vaguest transaction between them can and does take place. All it has to sustain it is a whisper, a bar of lost music, and a feeling hinting of an existence outside nature or this world where no leaves are.

In many ways "Credo" is like an Arnold poem, say "Dover Beach," though the narrative prelude of that poem, a device usually employed by Arnold, is missing. The mind in a moment of high seriousness, bent on a criticism of life, tells the bitter truth it has learned. But where the Arnold poem ends with man warring on a darkling plain, Robinson's counters the black and awful chaos of the night, the empirical truth, with the coming Light, a spiritually sensed power. The Robinson poem, like Arnold's, tells us something that can be said, and seems to be headed toward a generalization or a moral; but actually it turns off that course and ends, in effect, with a disclaimer, an acknowledgment of failure by the mind and a hint of something finer, too fine for the mind to grasp. A transaction has taken place, of course, for the poem is its product and embodiment, and the reader, observing the juxtaposition of statement and metaphor and accepting the poem into his consciousness as an aesthetic phenomenon, experiences that transaction directly himself.

Nevertheless the poem testifies to a schizophrenic division between the speaker's mind and soul. Lost in the black and awful chaos of the night, he hopefully awaits the light to show him his way. But his immediate condition is blindness, the world providing no clue to the meaning of its own or man's existence; things as they appear are meaningless. Unable to find his way, to act, or to be himself because he does not understand things, he can only passively give utterance to his plight and to his hope. During the same year "Credo" was published, Robinson wrote to Harry de Forest Smith,

66

. . . how the devil is a man to understand things in an age like this, when the whole trend of popular thought is in the wrong direction—not only that, but proud of the way it is taking. The age is all right, material progress is all right, Herbert Spencer is all right, hell is all right. These things are temporal necessities, but they are damned uninteresting to one who has caught a glimpse of the real light through the clouds of time. It is that glimpse that makes me wish to live and see it out.[47]

Here, though he is more specific about the nature of the darkness and the light, he still has had only a glimpse of the latter and still lives mainly on hope. The materialistic dualism has infiltrated into his very being and radically estranged his head from his heart.

"Credo" and the quoted letter imply the necessity and the hope of seeing life whole, for only with such comprehension can things be understood and man's way be clear. By the time of *The Man Against the Sky,* the first published volume of his second period, which extends to *Roman Bartholow,* Robinson no longer felt that it was possible to see life whole. Whereas in "Credo" the mind describes its predicament and states what will suffice, the title poem of *The Man Against the Sky* dramatizes the abortive attempt of the mind to arrive at ultimate meanings. In the poem the speaker, watching the silhouette of a man disappearing over a hill against the flaming sky of sunset, questions the meaning of life, then speculates on the possible answers. The point of view in *The Man Against the Sky* is still that of the remote observer-reflector, and the narrative structure again serves to trace the course of an intellectual act. The objectivity, still as pronounced, has taken a different form, however; the observer is able to identify himself with the figure he observes and thereby meditate on his own spiritual being as an externalized phenomenon. His attention has been directed away from himself, and so he runs much less risk of indulging in self-pity. As the loose ode structure of the poem suggests, the mind has become more empirical, open, and receptive; it doesn't simply feel an abstraction, the coming glory of the Light; it feels for something concrete, and so its relation with its subject has become more intimate. The poem is, appropriately, emotionally effusive.

As in "Credo," the intellectual effort to comprehend man's destiny fails: "Where was he going, this man against the sky?" the speaker asks near the end, and concludes, "You know not, nor do I" (66). This is the poem that Robinson said "came as near as anything to representing my poetic vision." [48] The point of view in "The Man Against the Sky" is, as in "Credo," the mind's, but the poem emphasizes the mind's quest to know rather than its statement of what will suffice. But as a statement of the truth, "The Man Against the Sky" does not differ from "Credo": neither proclaims the truth; one merely confesses to the mind's impotence, and the other merely presents the effort to attain the truth. A significant change has taken place, however. In "The Man Against the Sky" the mind, in acknowledging its impotence, admits that it is implicated in the world. The Light is not on its way; it can never determine life's meaning. All man can be certain of is the dramatic encounter between the mind and soul.

If this poem represents Robinson's poetic vision, that vision involves the inability of man ever to achieve an understanding of things. Robinson's glimpse of the real light through the clouds of time does not grow into a comfortable refuge, a certainty that protects him against things as they are. It does not allow him to escape time or life. The protagonist of *Merlin* (1917) speaks for this new sense of the relation between the mind and soul when he says,

> I saw too much when I saw Camelot;
> And I saw farther backward into Time,
> And forward, than a man may see and live,
> When I made Arthur king. I saw too far,
> But not so far as this. Fate played with me
> As I have played with Time; and Time, like me,
> Being less than Fate, will have on me his vengeance.
> On Fate there is no vengeance, even for God.   [297]

To be Merlin is to have a seer's power to know; but to know, finally and completely, is to understand that one is not outside of, but inextricably involved in, what is. The seer sees only what fate permits him to see and is just another instrument in the unfathomable progression and reach of events. Merlin, who felt he stood safely outside life and surveyed it aloofly, in the end realizes he has been caught in the web from the very beginning. He has been fate and time's fool, a tool of reality.

"The Man Against the Sky," a reflective monologue, is somewhat of an anomaly in the second stage of Robinson's career, when he found the dramatic monologue the most amenable form for his purposes. Because Browning had put his trademark on this form, it has been commonly assumed that Robinson, despite an expressed distaste for Browning's poetry and his insistence that it exercised no power over his imagination, borrowed a tailor-made device and did little more than play minor variations upon it. Actually Robinson, whose purposes were quite different from Browning's, used the form in a totally different way. Browning used the dramatic monologue to attain distance between himself and his subject, his readers and his characters.[49] He observes objectivity strictly, using irony as a major means for enforcing it. In a poem such as "My Last Duchess" poet and reader comically enjoy the Duke's vitality and unscrupulousness by remaining safely removed from his presence. This is made possible in part because both "have something on" the Duke, being able to see through his front to what he truly is. Neither can be fooled by his confidence game. They will not feel anything but will be cleverly analytical; their sharp intellects will protect them against the follies of sentiment.

Robinson used the dramatic monologue, on the other hand, to unite the mind and soul or to bring them together in greater communion. Perhaps Browning, consistently with Victorian sensibility, sought only to acknowledge and perpetuate the head's disengagement from the heart, but Robinson found this intolerable and, acting upon that impulse expressed in his looking forward to the coming of the light, sought to re-establish what Joseph Conrad referred to as solidarity. In "Ben Jonson Meets a Man from Stratford," for example, the speaker, Ben Jonson, is seriously dedicated to his subject, Shakespeare. His sincerity and deep feeling are trustworthy, so he leads us to become interested in and aggrieved about the suffering Shakespeare endures because of his double ambition. The bond between mind and soul suggested in "The Man Against the Sky" is much more overtly affirmed here. The dramatic monologue is used to emphasize interdependence between them, to engage the critical faculty with the life force. Not the estranged relation of "Credo" but a sympathetic, pragmatic relation has emerged.

The late long poems, beginning with *Roman Bartholow* (1923) and constituting Robinson's final period, are neither statements of the mind's plight and hope, as is "Credo," nor dramatizations of the mind's aggressive quest for understanding, as is "The Man Against the Sky"; rather, they are narratives of enlightenment. For example, Matthias, in *Matthias at the Door,* goes to the door of death after the collapse of his seemingly secure but actually rotten world to annihilate what little remains of his worthless life. Truth progressively eats away all the illusions upon which he has built his life until finally nothing remains but the wish to die. But at the door of death, through which all his acquaintances have easily passed, he is repulsed and told to live and build again. When he seeks an explanation for the command, asking "Where may the soul begin?" he is told, "If you could know, Matthias, you would be free. / But you are far from knowing, and are not free" (1151). Like the speaker of "The Man Against the Sky," Matthias is finally certain only of his ignorance and is sustained by a distant, ineffable light. Matthias cannot know the beginning and end of life, any more than could the speaker in "Credo" or "The Man Against the Sky," but he has received the command to live and he can believe in it.

Although the point of view in these long poems remains that of the mind, they are not, strictly speaking, intellectual acts. Matthias' attempt on occasion to make a statement or raise a question is squelched. The mind, as signified by the apparent absence of a narrator in the poem, has become passive, totally self-effacing, humble, and receptive. The poems have to be narrated by somebody, yet they give the appearance of being

70

dramas, a form without a narrator. In fact, however, the narrator is present, even though he has disappeared as the overtly present *I* so much in evidence in "Credo" and "The Man Against the Sky." Completely erasing itself, the mind, now an epiphenomenon of the soul, becomes a luminous absorber and articulator of spirit. Now it is truly objective, not interposing its own needs or anxieties but relating at great length the soul's struggle to be free. Significantly, its foreground subject is not dim feelings or silhouettes but concrete people. The narrative form, coupled with blank verse, has been expanded to incorporate an act larger than an intellectual effort to make statements or satisfy the need for conceptual truth, and, indeed, that expanded form frees the soul from a buried life. No longer complacent, as it was in "Maya," the mind by means of sympathy has become one with the soul, and the expanded form resulting from that sympathy provides the agency for the soul's liberation.

The inability of the mind to know the truth conceptually is a constant in Robinson's poetry from the beginning to the end of his career, but he was able to save himself from the fallen state imposed upon him by materialism by persisting in his desire to be whole again and finally achieving that wholeness, within the conditions life imposes, in his art. Accommodating his medium to reality, mainly by altering point of view and narrative structure—preferring, as Frost described it, the old ways of being new to the experimental ways—he became more concrete, if you will, about the spiritual but more obscure about the sensory and logical. He shadowed words with form so that the entire poem, through its structure and style, could be a living and final word capable of spelling the Word. The poem in its entirety having been transformed into a symbol, dense matter paradoxically lets in light. This is the major irony in a pervasively ironic poetry. The words Robinson inherited, in effect the material, like stone to the sculptor, out of which as a poet he was to make his art, are forced to reveal the truth of the spirit in spite of themselves. As he had to save himself from objectivity by being objective (that is, by eliminating the disjunctive effects of the objectifying faculty by purging himself

71

of egotism), so he had to make post-rationalistic poetry out of rational substances, turning words against themselves to do service in a cause contrary to their nature and being obscure so that he could concretely render the vital individual existent from an intellectual perspective in an intellective medium. With his imagination working, as it always does, to purify the dross from the natural world, of which the medium is a part, and from man, he cures himself of abstraction by, paradoxically, becoming yet more abstract—or by replacing intellectual abstractness with aesthetic concreteness.

Early in his career, while still subject to the influence of prosaic realism, he called "Luke Havergal," a poem in which a man stands at the Western gate listening to a voice from beyond the grave, an "uncomfortable abstraction," [50] and thereby revealed a theoretical malaise with subjects not realistic, that is, not empirically and socially concrete. The more he wrote, however, the more he was given to uncomfortable abstractions. As a poem about an individual struggling with matters separate from social life, "Luke Havergal" belongs to a conspicuous minority; but by the time Robinson wrote "The Man Against the Sky" he was quite comfortable with "abstractions." He was learning how to make these abstractions concrete. The late long poems bring to fulfillment the tendency uncomfortably present in "Luke Havergal" and more confidently treated in "The Man Against the Sky" and companion poems. These poems were devoted to examining man's nature and destiny independently of a social setting, and in them Robinson found a way to give the Truth of the spirit concrete embodiment. In effect, he replaced the epistemology of scientific empiricism with that of radical empiricism. He took consciousness as a legitimate province of knowledge. He then gave the conjunctive powers of the will and imagination precedence over the disjunctive ones of the intellect. As his epistemology changed, his task correspondingly became representation, not of external phenomena but of the human reality, not of what is seen but the power to see, and that entailed being true to inner being rather than to outer appearances. The late long poems, consequently, are narratives of the self concerned with the structure of prereflective experience, and in them observation and thought are subordinated to rendering the "subconscious life." [51]

The espousal of radical empiricism was not a departure from realism but was consistent with its principles. As William James did not repudiate science, so Robinson did not repudiate the desire to make poems that are true to life. In fact, in the last stage of his poetry he was even more explicitly concerned with being true to life than he was when he assumed an external comprehension of life to be possible. In the earlier poetry he limited himself to the phenomenal, but in the later poetry, where the new thought and cosmology has exerted its influence, he explicitly acknowledged this limitation as inescapable. Since, like James, Robinson limited himself to what is immediately, empirically, or existentially available, the adoption of radical empiricism did not bring with it transcendent knowledge, but only a more explicit, fuller understanding of the relation between the tangible and intangible in experience. Though it allowed the inner being of man to be taken seriously, and allowed Robinson to accommodate his medium to this subject, radical empiricism still required him to make poems that were true to life. His long poems, based on these conditions, are therefore realistic; however, because pure experience, not man as social being or as natural phenomenon, is their subject, they are realistic in the poetic rather than the prosaic sense.

In choosing an old way to be new Robinson wisely avoided falling into a dualism as invidious as the one he sought to escape. He could not resign himself to the realistic or naturalistic predicament that Henry James, Stephen Crane, Theodore Drieser, and others found it possible to live with. But he also rejected the lure of symbolism, a style, like realism and naturalism, based upon and perpetuating a dualism that radically separates the mind from the soul. Actually they are sibling styles, deriving from the same matrix, differing in that realism allows the soul to be banished from the scene and symbolism relies upon esoteric devices to fracture the mind's sterile concepts and deliver the living spirit into the world. They are, in other words, rivals in a war unto death between the mind and the soul. Symbolist poetry, as exemplified by Yeats and Eliot, even extends the dualism further than realism by divorcing the poet and the poem from the common reader. Its esoteric devices—symbols, myths, abstruse allusions, special learning, abstract and intellectual perspectives—reserve poetry for an artist-priesthood, an elite that takes refuge from the gross, vulgar, damned world in dogma and ritual accessible only to initiates.

Robinson avoided the symbolistic way of Yeats and Eliot, I think it is safe to say, because he instinctively sensed that it was antithetical to the way he must go. He didn't fail to write their kind of poetry because he didn't have the intelligence or talent for it. Like, for example, Joseph Conrad in *Lord Jim* and elsewhere, William Faulkner in *Absalom, Absalom,* William Carlos Williams in *Paterson,* Wallace Stevens in his poetry, or the major writers of poetry and fiction since World War II, he committed himself to achieving a unitive art. Accordingly, avoiding or eventually rejecting inherently dualistic styles, he made poetry out of the ordinary language of consciousness. Though the mind became a passive listener in his late poems, it almost always articulated the soul's truth in its own language, seldom in the cryptic or sacred language of the esoteric. In his poetry the soul, accepting the mind as its translator, can enter normal states of consciousness and everyday life, both of the individual and the community. His poetry can do so too. Furthermore, the poet and poetry do not become a special sect apart; accordingly, Robinson himself became a popular poet and still preserved his artistic integrity. In the only proper way for a poet, then, stylistically and structurally, Robinson created poems—poems of the earth, Wallace Stevens would call them—to make man whole again, and in doing so he was among the vanguard in the most important and enduring mode of thought and art in twentieth century America—the literature of integration.

The alienated self

Since we live only in and by contradictions, since life is tragedy and tragedy is
perpetual struggle, without victory or
the hope of victory, life is contradiction.

Miguel de Unamuno

Man, individual man, is the moral center of Robinson's
poetry. He begins with a nineteenth-century interest in character and carries over its corresponding ideal of the whole or
complete person. We know all too well that the twentieth century is the age of alienation, and alienated man can be found
with ease and in abundance in Robinson's poetry. Though
segregation and disintegration are there, to be sure, especially in
the early and middle poems but also as the starting point for the
later ones, they are not final but remediable conditions.
Robinson's treatment of his characters, particularly the course
of events he puts them through, is his most specific means for
displaying the achievement and meaning of integration.

Probably the most frequent "character" to appear in Robinson's poetry is Tilbury Town, the fictional community that
provides the setting for many of his poems and explicitly links
him and his poetry with small-town New England, the repressive, utilitarian social climate customarily designated as the
Puritan ethic. For Tilbury Town, more than simply a setting, is
an antagonistic moral force in the drama of life as Robinson
imagined it. In this capacity it is one pole in another aspect of
the dualism he inherited from materialism—the dichotomy be-

tween self and society, one more obstacle in the way to being whole.

The first reference to Tilbury Town occurs in "John Evereldown," which appeared in *The Torrent and the Night Before* (1896), Robinson's first volume of poetry. Here, simply a place, it has not yet acquired a dramatic role. In other poems of the same volume, however, the small-town community, though unnamed, does begin to assume such a role, as for instance in "Richard Cory," where the collective "we" speaks as a character. By the time of "Captain Craig" (1902) Tilbury Town is fully dressed for its part and firmly established as a dramatic persona. Here, from the beginning of the poem, the town is Captain Craig's explicit antagonist. The captain defines their differences this way:

> "Forget you not that he who in his work
> Would mount from these low roads of measured shame
> To tread the leagueless highways must fling first
> And fling forever more beyond his reach
> The shackles of a slave who doubts the sun.
> There is no servitude so fraudulent
> As of a sun-shut mind; for 'tis the mind
> That makes you craven or invincible,
> Diseased or puissant. The mind will pay
> Ten thousand fold and be the richer then
> To grant new service; but the world pays hard,
> And accurately sickens till in years
> The dole has eked its end and there is left
> What all of you are noting on all days
> In these Athenian streets, where squandered men
> Drag ruins of half-warriors to the grave—
> Or to Hippocrates." [166]

At issue, as the captain sees it, is the quality of life, with the two alternatives being the life-enhancing way of the sun-receptive mind and the life-squandering way of the world. The narrator of the poem, one of the few citizens of the town eventually to look after and listen to the captain, agrees with his views but even more explicitly criticizes the town when he remarks,

                                                    a few—
   Say five or six of us—had found somehow
   The spark in him, and we had fanned it there,
   Choked under, like a jest in Holy Writ,
   By Tilbury prudence.   [113]

Tilbury's prudence callously squanders life—literally, in this
instance—but the captain does not blame the town, or some
privileged faction of it, for his hard times; he is not interested in
criticizing prevailing institutions in order to bring about social
reform. Nor is the narrator, who writes,

   And he was right: there were no men to blame:
   There was just a false note in the Tilbury tune—
   A note that able-bodied men might sound
   Hosannas on while Captain Craig lay quiet.
   They might have made him sing by feeding him
   Till he should march again, but probably
   Such yielding would have jeopardized the rhythm;
   They found it more melodious to shout
   Right on, with unmolested adoration,
   To keep the tune as it had always been,
   To trust in God, and let the Captain starve. [114]

For both the captain and the narrator it is social or collective
man, whose interests are in getting on well materially rather
than in humanity or the quality of life, who is the object of their
criticism.

   By befriending the captain the narrator receives as reward
for his generous sympathy a rediscovery of an old truth, which
he states at the conclusion of his tale:

   The ways have scattered for us, and all things
   Have changed; and we have wisdom, I doubt not,
   More fit for the world's work than we had then;
   But neither parted roads nor cent per cent
   May starve quite out the child that lives in us—
   The Child that is the Man, the Mystery,
   The Phoenix of the World.   [168]

Throughout the poem, much is made of the child's consciousness as the source of spiritual health, or as the saving power,

and that consciousness is consistently linked with the imagery of light. Both the child and the light are excluded from Tilbury Town, and this repudiation of spirit is the town's most grievous sin. Its social materialism—its prudence, its righteousness and inhumanity, its "cent per cent" engrossment, its obsession with conventional worldly success—results in indifference to the captain as a suffering individual and to the eccentric, anticonformist ways of art, the soul, and the light for which he speaks. The town's prudence being a spiritual crassness and blindness that makes it an adamant enemy of the captain and what he values, the sun's light and the phoenix' fire are forever locked outside its walls.

Although Tilbury Town is not personified in "Captain Craig," as it is in "Richard Cory" and other poems where the collective "we" or a representative member is the speaker of the poem, "Captain Craig" provides the town with its biggest role. Never again does it rise to such explicit dramatic prominence. Yet whenever it appears thereafter, no matter how briefly, it bears the stamp of the spiritual crassness and blindness suggested in "Richard Cory" and fully and explicitly defined in "Captain Craig." For example, in "Isaac and Archibald," two old men of rough but ready friendship unconsciously instruct a boy, the narrator, in the ways of humanity, but that instruction takes place outside the town, as it must. And never again is Tilbury Town simply a place; it is always a character, the collective consciousness, antagonist of the peculiar, gifted, or farseeing individual, who, a failure by conventional standards, dedicates himself to the interior life.

Although Tilbury Town, easily identified with Gardiner, Maine, is the most direct device Robinson could use for treating the individual's alienation from the community, it is not his only one. Shakespeare's obsession with Stratford and Rembrandt's troubles with Amsterdam, as well as St. Paul's with Rome, the Wandering Jew's with New York, and Merlin's and Lancelot's with Camelot are vehicles for the same theme. In fact, as this brief list suggests, Robinson's better known poems are usually on this subject. His personal troubles [1] permitted him to imagine

concrete and profound images of men caught in a sharp antagonism between the radically opposed values of poetry and materialism, whether the men were citizens of Tilbury Town, artists,
religious men, or knights. He knew intimately the hostility of
a money-based society to poetry. Its investment in superficial
outer signs of power such as property and wealth precluded
tolerance for the human spirit, and so drove a deep wedge
between man's interior life and his outer social world. As a poet,
as a spokesman for the life of the spirit in a materialistic society,
he knew the social dualism challenged him to fight for his life.

Tilbury Town is the most direct geographical embodiment
of Robinson's antagonism toward a materialistic community
antipathetic to spirit, and "Captain Craig" is his largest dramatic rendering of that antipathy. But his most subtle and
profound treatments of it are found in his deservedly well-
known medium-length poems on the artist, in, for example,
"Ben Jonson Entertains a Man from Stratford" and "Rembrandt to Rembrandt." Ben Jonson says of Shakespeare, in
defining the source of his black depression, that "there's the
Stratford in him; he denies it, / And there's the Shakespeare in
him" (21). "Manor-bitten to the bone" (23) and at the same
time "Lord Apollo's homesick emissary" (21), Shakespeare is
torn between the contrary pulls of these two sides of his being.
In trying to account for the hold of "that House in Stratford"
(32) on Shakespeare, Jonson thinks Shakespeare is racked by

> . . . the fiery art that has no mercy
> But what's in that prodigious grand new House.
> I gather something happening in his boyhood
> Fulfilled him with a boy's determination
> To make all Stratford 'ware of him.   [27]

The insights that art has made available to him have revealed to
Shakespeare that all is worthless, even his ambition for the
house, yet the demon driving him to be a citizen of rank in
Stratford will not allow him freedom from this obsession.

In Shakespeare the conflict is internalized, as it was personally for Robinson, so that he is the victim of the mutual
animosity of both sides. Rembrandt, though he is caught in the

79

same countercurrents, has a better time of it in that he makes
the choice of art at the sacrifice of his fame and fortune in
Holland and becomes free of the rending antagonisms within
himself. "Sometimes a personage in Amsterdam / But now not
much" (587), his "Me" addresses his "I," [2] represented by his
self-portrait on the canvas:

> That was a fall, my friend, we had together—
> Or rather it was my house, mine alone,
> That fell, leaving you safe. Be glad of that.
> There's life in you that shall outlive my clay
> That's for a time alive and will in time
> Be nothing—but not yet. You that are there
> Where I have painted you are safe enough
>   . . . [586]

As always with Robinson, this life, like the fire in Shakespeare's
art, is the life of the spirit:

> We know together of a golden flood
> That with its overflow shall drown away
> The dikes that held it; and we know thereby
> That in its rising light there lives a fire
> No devils that are lodging here in Holland
> Shall put out wholly, or much agitate,
> Except in official preparation
> They put out first the sun.   [587]

Holland's scorn had frightened Rembrandt into submission and
thus into self-denial, but latterly he had come to recognize the
cost of his submission, which was

> The taste of death in life—which is the food
> Of art that has betrayed itself alive
> And is the food of hell.   [585]

And so he realizes that his life lies in his being and destiny as an
artist:

>   Whether I would
> Or not, I must; and here we are as one
> With our necessity . . . . [587]
> . . . .
> You are the servant, Rembrandt, not the master,—
> But you are not assigned with other slaves

80

That in their freedom are the most in fear.
One of the few that are so fortunate
As to be told their task and to be given
A skill to do it with, a tool too keen
For timid safety . . .   [590]

The price of being true to himself is ostracism and banishment; he has to go forth alone into the darkness, with his only solace being that "if you are right / Others will have to see" (590).

These two poems reveal that even the most concrete representation of the conflict between self and society, which begins with an antagonism between an artist's worldly ambition and his devotion to his art, transcends the psychological and moral issue of art versus materialism and becomes an antipathy inherent in the dualistic nature of life. Two aspects of life, two realities, are pitted in eternal hostility, and when caught between them, a man's vital being is torn apart. When he chooses between them, he must pay the price of either self-betrayal or exclusion from the human community. There are two truths and each abhors the other, so that man is trapped in a dilemma in which every gain automatically entails a loss; every joy, suffering, no matter what choice he makes.

Other poems more explicitly universalize the alienation of self and society. In them the hostility is objectified even more than it is in "Rembrandt to Rembrandt": the antagonists become separate entities that stand over against one another. Both Rembrandt and Shakespeare are instances of inner conflict, which one man resolves and the other does not. But this is not so in the "Wandering Jew" (456–59), where a mythic figure angrily battles the society in which he finds himself—New York in this case. The narrator of the poem, an adult, reveals the nature of the Wandering Jew when he says, "I had known / His image when I was a child"; with "Captain Craig" as evidence, it is clear that this link with childhood connects the Wandering Jew with the Light. Robinson emphasizes the Wandering Jew's "loneliness" and the tragic dualism by asserting that "the figure and the scene / Were never to be reconciled." When he goes on to say that the Wandering Jew's eyes at times seem to look on a

81

"Presence . . . One who never dies. / For such a moment he revealed / What life has in it to be lost," there can indeed be no doubt that the Wandering Jew represents the spirit in a spiritually desiccated world. Thus his very existence is "an angry task / That relegates him out of time / To chaos," and he knows with bitterness the "many a lonely time in vain / The Second Coming came and went." He is quite aware that he is doomed to failure in his task, and though his "old, unyielding eyes may flash" when he by chance comes face to face with another person, they will "flinch—and look the other way"; he knows that he can never enter society, that he is forever excluded from the human community, and that the waters of the spirit can never revive the arid "scene."

In "The Wandering Jew," where the protagonist is a mythical figure, myth replaces art as the enemy of society, the two being at heart the same, of course, except that myth is more inclusive. No longer do art and materialism simply offer a choice of contrasting values, if that is all they ever did; now they are clearly but one form of a much larger conflict. And that conflict extends even beyond myth and society: a still more inclusive form of it, found in such poems as "Three Taverns" and "Nicodemus," is the hostility between the religious experience and the social forms of religion—dogma and the church. In a critical remark on Gardiner, Robinson asked when the human race would acquire anything like a logical notion of human life, then added, "or, in other words, of Christianity." [3] These two poems could be regarded as his view of Christianity in Gardiner, and it is significant that Christ, though his presence haunts the poems, never actually appears. They can also be regarded as portrayals of the alienation of spirit, the ultimate human reality, from society.

In "Three Taverns" St. Paul says that he had "had men slain / For saying Something was beyond the Law, / And in ourselves" (462) when he had been an orthodox Jew. But after his religious experience on the road to Damascus, he looks back upon his past and concludes he was "A prisoner of the Law, and of the Lord / A voice made free" (462). St. Paul tells his audience that now, after his conversion, "The man you see not— / The man within the man—is most alive" (463). And in finding his spiritual being he has "lost all else / For wisdom, and the wealth of it" (470) and is a "criminal . . . for seeing beyond the law / That which the Law saw not" (471). Though aware that he is a criminal and will be executed if apprehended, he nevertheless intends to enter Rome for the inevitable tragic encounter with entrenched authority. His religious experience has given him the terrible knowledge that the spirit, "the man within the man," is the radical enemy of social forms, religious and otherwise.

The antagonism between the mystical inner reality and society is stated in its most general form by Robinson at the end of *Lancelot*—though the antagonism must be understood to include personal relations (that of lovers, in this case) as well as that of an individual to a group. Here Robinson writes of Lancelot,

> . . . he rode on, under the stars,
> Out of the world, into he knew not what,
> Until a vision chilled him and he saw,
> Now as in Camelot, long ago in the garden,
> The face of Galahad who had seen and died,
> And was alive now in a mist of gold.
> He rode on into the dark, under the stars,
> And there were no more faces. There was nothing.
> But always in the darkness he rode on,
> Alone; and in the darkness came the Light. [449]

The Light and the world are not simultaneously available to man; he must choose between them; and what is finally at stake in that choice is life and death. As Nicodemus expresses it in an impassioned argument against Caiaphas, who defends the Law,

> You are a priest of death, not knowing it.
> There is no life in those old laws of ours,
> Caiaphas; they are forms and rules and fears,
> So venerable and impressive and majestic
> That we forget how little there is in them

For us to love. We are afraid of them.
They are the laws of death; and, Caiaphas,
They are the dead who are afraid of dying.   [1164]

Shakespeare's black depression, the Wandering Jew's anger, Rembrandt's and St. Paul's risking all for the Light, Nicodemus' impassioned attack—all reveal how the man with special knowledge of the spirit's truth reacts to society, to life in death. Inherent in man is a hostility between inner being and external forms and relations, between what Emerson called "the instantaneous in-streaming causing power" [4] and the objects that can hinder or misdirect its flowing.

Despite his obvious sympathies with the spirit, Robinson never assumes an immediate or long-run triumph by the self over society in which social forms are "saved." As with every subject, his concern for truth led him to adopt an objective attitude toward the relation between self and society; he simply records from various points of view and with varying results things as they are, the simultaneous presence and irreconcilability of self with society. Rembrandt chooses art and is free; Shakespeare cannot choose and suffers; St. Paul discovers the inner man and is doomed; Nicodemus recognizes the truth but is impotent; the Wandering Jew is the truth, but he too is impotent. Richard Cory is viewed from the point of view of the town; the town is viewed from the point of view of Eben Flood. The first dies tragically; the second lives comically. Lancelot rides out of the world, but in the long poems after *Lancelot* the protagonist—for example, Fargo of *Amaranth,* who abandons art to become a plumber—in effect returns to the world. But in every poem, regardless of what happens, the initial truth, the given condition of human existence, is the alienation of self from society, a schism between art and social values, the spirit and social forms, the soul and doctrine, the Light and the world. And finally that schism is an irremediable dichotomy in man's being between his personal and his social self. The pressure of creative power against achieved form is never more than momentarily relaxed.

The materialism Robinson set out to reject not only killed

nature but also threatened to socialize man. To preserve the uniquely human from metaphysical materialism, Robinson had to dissociate man from nature; to preserve it from "social materialism," he had to dissociate the self from society. Thus in getting rid of materialism Robinson sought to free the spirit from antispiritual society as well as from nature by giving the spirit an autonomous existence beyond both. William Barrett remarks, "It has become a law of modern society that man is assimilated more and more completely to his social function," [5] and this succinctly describes the social development that Robinson, in addition to the epistemological and aesthetics problems previously cited, had to find a solution to in order to achieve his desired unity. Robinson struggled for integration and eventually attained it, but in his early and middle poetry not the integration but the disintegration of the individual from the group, the external world, and himself is emphasized.

Nowhere are the effects of alienation more apparent than in one of Robinson's favorite characters, the empowered person who can help others but not himself. Bearer of the secret knowledge of the spirit, he can see what others are blind to and work mysterious effects on their lives, but as a bearer of that knowledge he, like Rembrandt, is outlawed from intimate human relations and the human community. His knowledge bars him from worldly position and power, for having broken through to the higher truth, he can never take any social role seriously, and so can never do anything for himself as a social creature.

The empowered person's predicament, Robinson saw, is only one instance of the plight of the "I" in every man. If the "I" and the "Me" are antithetical aspects of life and self, how can they communicate with and tolerate one another? How can man survive as man? For if the "I" is "unsocializable," then communication and harmony between the "I" and "Me" are impossible. And if they are impossible, so is poetry, for it would be impossible to affirm consciously the "I" in aesthetic as well as discursive terms, art being a consciously created public object. In fact, the spirit, if it can be said ever to have existed, could not be known and would perish from neglect. Robinson sensed that separateness, hostility, alienation cannot be the whole truth, therefore; something beyond and encompassing division unites apparent antitheses.

The empowered person who can help others but not himself exemplifies all the problems resulting from the alienated self, including those arising from the relation of man to society, to man, and to himself. And his predicament, finally, raises all the nasty problems of communication, which strike right to the heart of the poet's responsibilities when he is as socially conscious as Robinson was. Robinson mulls these problems over again and again, considering them from varying perspectives and under various conditions. One of his best known poems on the subject is "Eros Turannos," which treats of human isolation in its most extreme form. Here, a woman, betrayed by the man she was depending upon to protect her against the "downward years" and estranged from the town where she lives, is divested of her illusions of love and is thrown back upon the terrible truth of her being. Commenting on her experience, the narrator, the collective "We," remarks:

> We tell you, tapping on our brows,
>   The story as it should be,—
> As if the story of a house
>   Were told, or ever could be;
> We'll have no kindly veil between
> Her visions and those we have seen,—
> As if we guessed what hers have been,
>   Or what they are or would be.
>
> Meanwhile we do no harm; for they
>   That with a god have striven,
> Not hearing much of what we say;
>   Take what the god has given . . .   [33]

The story of a house—symbol for an individual's life—cannot be told; the depth where an individual strives with the gods cannot be plumbed by another, whether the "We" be the collective consciousness or a storyteller. The poem asserts that the existential level of experience, which is the spirit's region, is inaccessible not only to the intellect ("our brows") but also to art. Under any and all circumstances it is true that, as Matthias

86

says, "No man has known another / Since men were born" (1133). The man-within-the-man St. Paul spoke of is doomed to eternal isolation. Man is indeed alone.

If "Eros Turannos" tells the whole truth, man, society, and poetry could not exist as we know them, because there would be no way for the spirit to enter the world, society, or consciousness; and if it cannot enter these, then all of life is reduced to inert matter, and materialism is triumphant. But society, man, and the self do survive, however precariously. For Robinson the spirit does enter into the world and communication between men and within man does take place. Captain Craig, for instance, argues at great length that this communication is the mission of the poet and poetry. The empowered person who can help others but not himself is another instance of such communication. In "Captain Craig," a poem that is typical of a form Robinson uses also in "Isaac and Archibald," "Flammonde," and "The Man Who Died Twice," a narrator who apprehends with his conscious intellectual faculties tells the story of his encounter with an eccentric character who lives by a deeper spiritual awareness. The eccentric communicates his awareness to the narrator so that in the end the narrator's life is deepened. Although Captain Craig dies without altering the quality of life in Tilbury Town and is in part killed by the town's indifference, he does have influence; he produces a spiritual enhancement, an enlargement of consciousness, in the lives of five or six of its citizens. This transaction, as slight and vague as it may be, results in a dim self-discovery, enough to awaken and sustain the spirit.

Although the spirit can enter society, it can do so only at specific points and temporarily. Society as a whole, antithetical by nature to spirit, is not itself redeemable. The spirit enters only through specific persons, only in a dialogue between men, and is communicable only between individuals. And then it cannot enter directly or be straightforwardly communicated; it can enter only indirectly through an infinitesimal gap provided by compassion, the glint of eyes, or the tone of voice. The narrator of "Captain Craig" asserts that he and his friends could have been "wrecked on [the Captain's] own abstractions" (167) had they taken the captain's words for the Word; the narrator of "The Man Who Died Twice," though he professes to believe, cannot be sure that Fernando Nash's claims about the meaning of his mystical experience are true; and the Wandering Jew, Ponce de Leon, Rembrandt, and numerous others communicate spiritually through their eyes, not through language. Not negotiable through words or institutions, the transaction between man and man occurs obliquely. But it does occur, and with God and nature dead, this silent dialogue is the sole means by which the special knowledge of the "seer" can enter the consciousness of a normal person and the "I" can become known to the conscious mind.

It seems somewhat paradoxical that Robinson emphasizes the dialogue between man and man, which is a social relation, and denigrates society so thoroughly. But there is no paradox: the dialogue simply takes place on two levels, those of the "I" and the "Me." On the level of the "Me" the dialogue amounts to an exchange of acquired attitudes associated with roles, while on the level of the "I" it amounts to awakening the underground, personal, religious self. Little of value and much that is harmful is transferred in the communication between "Me's," whereas the existence, integrity, and realization of the spirit is made possible through the communication between "I's." It is for this reason that Robinson so heavily emphasizes the value of compassion, explicitly in "Zola" and implicitly in the poems in which a narrator, a sympathetic observer and listener, discovers his own deeper reaches through a seer.

And it is also for this reason that he returns repeatedly to the subject of guilt, which as he conceives it is the betrayal, not of God by man, but of man by man. A great number of his poems—"Bokardo," "Avon's Harvest," "Sisera," "Cavender's House," "King Jasper," for example—are devoted in whole or in large part to rendering the destructive effects of guilt on the self. Guilt, of course, presupposes conscience, and for Robinson conscience is a moral sense innate in the "I," for which the primary moral value is the sanctity of the individual person. In

"Sisera," Jael for her own aggrandizement has treacherously killed Sisera while he slept. "Tell Deborah," she exultantly proclaims, "that a woman, / A woman filled with God, killed Sisera / For love of Israel" (1178). And she defends her act with the argument, "What is one man, or one man's way of dying, / So long as Israel has no more of him" (1177). A man is of no significance; Israel and God, superhuman entities, justify sacrificing him should one choose to serve them and seek their rewards. Everyone else in the poem, however, though impotent before an orthodox devotion to God and country, clearly reacts with horror and disgust to what Jael has done. Through vanity, the enemy of compassion, she destroys the bond between man and man, and thereby loses her humanity, the very life of the spirit that she ironically affirms in placing the murdered Sisera at the feet of God and Israel. By betraying another she betrays herself.

A way to testify to the spirit's existence and a means by which to release it more liberally into society and the "Me," greater communication through rejecting the abstract and valuing the concrete: these were the desiderata issuing for Robinson from the self's alienation. Their attainment had to wait until the later poems, however. In a sonnet on Erasmus, the major historical figure in humanism, Robinson wrote,

> When he protested, not too solemnly,
> That for a world's achieving maintenance
> The crust of overdone divinity
> Lacked ailment, they called it recreance;
> And when he chose through his own glass to scan
> Sick Europe, and reduced, unyieldingly,
> The monk within the cassock to the man
> Within the monk, they called it heresy.
>
> And when he made so perilously bold
> As to be scattered forth in black and white,
> Good fathers looked askance at him and rolled
> Their inward eyes in anguish and affright;
> There were some of them did shake at what was told
> And they shook best who knew that he was right.
> [193]

89

He is, of course, speaking for himself, although his target was society and sick America rather than the church and sick Europe: he protested against the crust of overdone socialization, and he reduced man to "the man within the man." He was not a romantic; he did not assume that paradise would be regained by returning to a natural state; rather, he felt, like Hawthorne, that social existence is prerequisite to humanity and requires the compromise of individual aberrations. But society itself, he recognized, suffers from severe limitations. By its very nature it is incapable of honoring and encouraging the individual or the man within the man. Of course, society is only the behavior of individuals in relation to one another, so that what the term actually refers to is the tendency of human beings to deny their spiritual being and that of others by preferring the social to the spiritual bond between men. Robinson acknowledged that it is only natural, therefore, that society and spirit be permanently at odds; they are radical alternatives within the self that the individual must choose between and take the consequences, as Rembrandt or any other artist must choose between the fashionable public taste and his own vision. And it is obvious that should an individual pursue economic or social ends—wealth, status, power, etc.—he must perforce neglect his soul. Society or social values are thus antithetical to humanistic ones, and the true bond between men, instead of being a social relation of "Me's," is a relation of "I's" based on identity, compassion, and conscience. Humanism, as it is commonly understood, simultaneously affirms man's dignity and accepts his limitations. With Robinson, this ambiguity takes the form of honoring the marvelous and mysterious spiritual life in man and recognizing that man is human only when he is moral, when, that is, he repudiates egotism and lives in accordance with his responsibility to man. The forces that produce society and the "Me," the instruments of socialization, block communication and the life of the spirit; but regardless how hidden that life must be or how estranged from society, the private, personal, presocial elements in experience do exist and are expressed, and man is thereby saved from social totalitarianism.

Robinson's most felicitous treatment of alienation is "Flammonde" (1-6), which states, more precisely and profoundly than any of his other poems, the multidimensions and full consequences (the central myth, it might be called) in the self's journey toward truth, at the stage before that journey can be completed. Yvor Winters, an avid admirer of Robinson's poetry, discarded "Flammonde" from the Robinson canon because it was "repulsively sentimental," [6] and his criticism of the poem as unadulterated romanticism would seem to be supported by biographical fact. It did result from storybook inspiration: "While sitting in a movie theatre," Robinson said, "suddenly I saw Flammonde and I could hear the poem quite clearly. All the lines were there and I only had to write them down." [7] But this romantic origin, this gift from the unconscious, could mean that this "spontaneous" creation represents in its deepest or truest form Robinson's own sense of life.

The poem is ostensibly about Flammonde, or more precisely, "the man Flammonde." He is one of those gifted persons ("Rarely at once will nature give / The power to be Flammonde and live") who sees but cannot do for himself. He comes for a brief sojourn in Tilbury Town, where in appearance and demeanor he is everything that its citizens are not; no one knows where he came from or where he went, only that he is characterized by a "firm address and foreign air"; has the "news of nations in his talk / And something royal in his walk"; a "glint of iron in his eyes / But never doubt, nor yet surprise"; stands "Erect, with his alert repose / About him, and about his clothes." He appears "As one by kings accredited." While he is in Tilbury Town Flammonde befriends a disgraced woman, recognizes the intellectual ability of a boy and provides for his education, and joins old enemies in friendship, among other good works. Through his superior vision and power he sees more deeply into men and is able to work wonders among a few individual citizens of the town by introducing an unaccustomed compassion and humanity into their lives. That is the man in Flammonde. But he is indeed an unusual man, for if he is a man at all, he is the essential spiritual being and power of man. As his name "the flame of the earth" implies, he is, like the Wandering Jew, a mythological figure. His flame, along with the glint of iron in his eyes and everything else about him, establishes him as an envoy of the Light who comes out of nowhere ("God knows where") into a community of futile people to work his wonders, then disappears without a trace. It is impossible for the townsmen to tell whether he is playing a role (assuming a "Me" as the "Prince of Castaways") or is genuine; but despite their uncertainty, he brings the Light, the mystic power, for a brief moment, redeeming a portion of the impotent community by introducing into it the capacity for creative action for good.

Flammonde is not, however, the subject of the poem: more properly, the subject, to take advantage of the pun, is the narrator's consciousness; Flammonde is the object. The poem is about the narrator's attempt to understand what Flammonde was; it is a dramatization in which the mind meets and interacts with the soul, the "Me" meets and interacts with the "I." The broad structural outlines of the poem are sufficient testimony of this. The first three stanzas describe Flammonde, and thus fix an image of him before the narrator's and the reader's eyes; the next five recount his exploits and reveal his powers; the concluding four are devoted to reflection upon what Flammonde was. The poem is a meditation in which the eyes fix themselves on an image while the mind, working upon the image, tries to comprehend its significance. And this is an action of consciousness in which awareness proceeds from its simplest form, sensory perception, to its higher forms.

But to understand what is involved in the higher forms of awareness, it is necessary to look much closer at what happens in the poem. In the first place, the narrator is trying to answer his question about Flammonde some time after his appearance in Tilbury Town, so that the narrator is not conducting an empirical investigation but is working on material provided by his memory, the storehouse of the impressions Flammonde made upon him. Sensory perception was the means of the narrator's acquaintance with Flammonde, the source of the "contact"

of his consciousness with him, but during perception no understanding took place, only the awareness of physical features,
bearing, and behavior. Although the conscious transaction between the speaker and Flammonde during perception was limited to appearances, the narrator was *touched* in the depths of
his being, and in time this unconscious depth response erupts
into the conscious through unabetted recollection. As the narrator says,

> We cannot know how much we learn
> From those who never will return,
> Until a flash of unforeseen
> Remembrance falls on what has been.

Apparently the mysterious and strangely powerful man has set
astir something in the darker recesses of the narrator's being.
Perhaps a power present but not detected in the sensory images
awakens his "I" through resonance. In time these aspects of his
self gather force and emerge from darkness; then they are available for the reflective mind to ponder. It is at this moment and
for this purpose that the narrator writes the poem, seeking an
answer to the haunting question of who Flammonde was.

His question is obviously misplaced; it is not Flammonde
but that part of his own being brought disturbingly alive by
Flammonde that the narrator wants to understand. But, typically for Robinson, the "I" is viewed objectively, and so the
narrator's attention is directed away from introspection toward
an objectified, mythological embodiment of his inner being. He
must work from the outside to the inside, and to go in that
direction is not to go very far. The inescapable consequence is
the inability of the narrator to answer his question; Flammonde
remains unknown, a mystery. But that isn't the complete story:
intellectual comprehension fails, true, but a transaction has
taken place, as the narrator's writing of the poem testifies, and
as the narrator points out when he says in conclusion that "from
time to time/ In Tilbury Town, we look beyond / Horizons for
the man Flammonde." Tilbury Town has not been redeemed
once and for all, but it has been made aware that something

exists beyond its horizons. Although Tilbury Town and Flammonde are not permanently compatible, communication has taken place between them and the "We" has become aware—dimily, to be sure—of the deeper, hidden life of the spirit.

Such are the form, the dynamics, and the consequences of the meeting of self and society in "Flammonde." It should be noted that the meeting takes place on three levels: between an individual and the community (Flammonde and Tilbury Town); between man and man (Flammonde and the narrator); and between the "I" and the "Me" of the narrator. It is also of significance that Flammonde is linked with the cleansing heritage of tradition, which is collective memory, and that tradition represents the endurance of spirit through history, while society, with no roots outside of time or permanence within it, is caught in the flux of endless, meaningless change. Because self transcends society and the corrosive effects of time, it is also beyond conventional morality, and therefore Flammonde cannot be ethically judged. His was a hero's or a saint's fate, his vocation being with the divine, not with man, except when, Christlike, he passed through a community as bearer of the Word and left behind him a dim wake of Light. When that Light awakens some men spiritually, they are driven to ponder what lies beyond death as they continue their climb up the darkening hill of life. But Flammonde must continue on his way, enduring his special fate of wandering the earth like a bonze, alone and alienated. Though he possessed mythic power and exercised it, he could not escape his fate. What he accomplished was done by juxtaposition and resonance, not by overt words or force of will. He can never directly offer his gift, and he can never turn it to his own advantage.

Robinson's primary "myth," then, traces the soul's journey to self-awareness, under the conditions life provides and to the degree possible up to and during the time he wrote almost all the poems discussed in this chapter. At this point the alienated self, as in "Captain Craig," is still on the defensive. An aggressive society expels it, or an eager mind reaches out to grasp it.

Shy and self-defensive, the self warily moves about the periphery and eludes its pursuer, waiting for conditions more favorable to it. The animosity here is sharp, but Robinson is not done with psychological probing: he has not yet taken his characters as far as they can and will have to go.

Man as he actually is

Freedom, to be plain, is nothing but

THE INSIDE OF THE OUTSIDE

Joyce Cary

Given the alienated self, in order to escape materialism and find a belief to live by, Robinson had not only to elude the debilitating effects resulting from the divisions between thought and being, and language and reality, but those resulting from the division between self and society as well. Though latent in his earlier work, his manner of escaping from the latter dualism is not fully attained until the late long poems from *Roman Bartholow* (1927) to *King Jasper* (1937). In them he arrives at his final truth about man as he actually is.

Those who have emphasized Robinson's thought have over-looked or slighted his turning to the long poem, preferring in the most extreme instances to consider it an unfortunate whim of a poet whose "ideas" had remained the same but who could not resist the temptation of fame and fortune.[1] But Robinson did not consider it so. While writing his long poems, he re-marked about short ones, "They don't come anymore";[2] and on a later occasion, speaking of the long poems he had already written, he said, "Anyhow, I had to do them."[3] He apparently submitted to the dictates of inspiration and felt that when the subject—in Henry James's sense[4]—took possession of the poet's imagination, the poet had no choice in the general form of its expression. "If a man has something worth saying," Robinson remarked, criticizing experimental poetry, "the character of its expression will come out of its content; but some of these new fellows have so little to say that the manner of expression is an assumed one. It doesn't grow out of its material." [5] When form is equated with content in this manner, it is not a vehicle for the literary idea, but is itself that idea. A change in form is a change in "thought," and since the late long poems are clearly different in form from the rest of Robinson's poetry, they must assert their own unique and particular truth.

The formal differences of these poems in point of view and narrative structure have already been commented on. In addition, there are decisive changes in tone, style, and theme. The comic mood, rather frequent in his early poetry and natural to his objectivity during that period, gives way to an almost unrelieved somberness; the playful exuberance of "Captain Craig," for example, is replaced by straightforward Arnoldian high seriousness. Life is not so ludicrous for Robinson when he is engaged in it, and certainly the truth of the self is not revealed with the scoffing attitude that he favored in his early poems. Sincerity, compassion, and responsibility, the prerequisites for receiving that truth, set the dominant mood. As his attention focused more closely on the self, Robinson experimented with hallucinations, dreams, and symbolism. His language became less colloquial and more abstract and literary, and his poetry, accordingly, is more and more characterized by a deficiency he cited in "Captain Craig"—"prosiness." [6] His characters become less vividly distinguished as individuals, and the action in his stories becomes more involuted and obscure than before, until, as Yvor Winters noted, the long poems become so vague as to require at least one reading just to determine what takes place in them.

One of the least obvious signs indicating that new ideas are embodied in the late long poems is the change in emphasis in Robinson's attitude toward the child. In "Captain Craig" the child had a position of high moral import. There, the narrator notes at the end of his tale that we may not "starve quite out the child that lives in us, / The Child that is the Man, the Mystery, / The Phoenix of the World" (168). In this early long poem and elsewhere in his early work—for example, in the

97

title poem of his second volume, *The Children of the Night*—
Robinson favored identifying man's spiritual being with the
child. He did so partly because man appeared to him small and
impotent in a vast, dark universe where he was beyond the
reach of his Father's voice. But in "Captain Craig" and generally, Robinson was attracted to the child for the same reason
that many Romantics and Victorians before him were—because
the child, in his pristine awareness, trailing clouds of glory, was
thought to be still close to his spiritual origins. His soul unal-
loyed, uncontaminated by the gross world, the child represented
the saving remnant of spirit in man. However, from another
point of view the child's innocence turns into naiveté, ignorance
about life's terrible complexity and difficulty. Robinson's enthusiasm for the child in "Captain Craig" sprang from his feeling
then that if the spirit could keep from becoming involved in the
world, it could remain pure and whole. To the end of his career
Robinson continued to regard this side of the child's awareness
with respect, and wrote in his last poem, *King Jasper*, "Who
knows a child, knows God" (1417). But his progress from
objective detachment to *engagement* inextricably bound the
spirit to the world, and once implicated in life it could not
escape adult intellectual and moral awareness. Thus in "Hill-
crest," a poem written about fifteen years after "Captain Craig,"
Robinson was considerably less enthusiastic about the child's
virtues:

> Who sees unchastened here the soul
> Triumphant has no other sight
> Than has a child who sees the whole
> World radiant with its own delight.   [17]

And in "The Three Taverns," published in 1920, he was still
mainly conscious of the way in which the soul has to earn its
light through suffering:

> The fire that smites
> A few on highways, changing all at once
> Is not for all. The power that holds the world
> Away from God that holds himself away—
> . . . .

> Was not, or ever shall be, a small hazard
> Enlivening the ways of easy leisure
> Or the cold road of knowledge.   [466]

Obviously as Robinson grew away from his own childhood, he fell from innocence; and in a fallen state he could not regard spiritual awareness as merely a gift. The soul must be endowed, certainly, but it also must be chastened through pain and sacrifice. For this reason the child, who appears rather frequently in his early poems, disappears from the late poetry except for a couple of passing allusions.

This change in Robinson's attitude toward the child, however, is relatively superficial compared to the transformation in his attitude toward thought and will. In his early poetry Robinson designates the ultimate spiritual reality as "Thought"—as, for example, in these lines from "Two Quatrains":

> As eons of incalculable strife
> Are in the vision of one moment caught,
> So are the common, concrete things of life
> Divinely shadowed on the walls of Thought.
> [107]

At this time Robinson on occasion called himself an idealist, accepting the assumption that man and reality are rational and locating man's spiritual being in his conscious faculties. Later "thought" disappears from Robinson's vocabulary and is replaced by "power" and "will," the first of which occurs in the opening passage of *Roman Bartholow,* where Roman is portrayed as awakening to a new life:

> he might
> This morning have addressed a votive shout,
> Affirming his emergence, to the Power
> That filled him as light fills a buried room
> When earth is lifted and the sun comes in.
> [733]

The second occurs in "Maya":

> The soul of man went up to a far height;
> And where those others would have had no sight
> Or sense of else than terror for the blind,
> Soul met the Will . . .   [872]

99

At this later time Robinson turned to a voluntarism which locates the source of life and action in the unconscious or suprara-
tional. When he conceived of reality as thought, he tended to
regard it as a fixed order of eternal forms that can be rationally
comprehended; when he conceived of it as power or will, it
became a process, a ceaseless force of destruction and construc-
tion that never attaches itself permanently to any given order.

Thought and power or will are the ultimate terms, the
metaphysical dimensions, of the pervasive dualism Robinson
struggled against, and his shift of allegiance from the former to
the latter marks indelibly a change of mind on his part during
his career. Because Robinson has been a victim of the cliché
that American writers don't grow, his reputation, such as it is,
rests entirely upon the shorter poems of his early and middle
period. If any of the long poems are praised at all, it is usually
the Arthurian ones, while the others have been consistently
ignored. Taste has undoubtedly been a determinant here, for it
is in the shorter poems of the early and especially the middle
period and the Arthurian poems that Robinson comes closest to
the kind of poetry preferred by the New Critics. Based on a
sharp strain between self and society or the Light and the world,
they are characterized by the ambiguity, tension, and irony we
have of late been taught to value in art, though somewhat more
in theme than in overt style. But much of the explanation for
their low reputation comes simply from their being long poems,
which are discriminated against by contemporary taste in general because they demand a poetic response we are unaccustomed to today. Romanticism established the principle that true
poetry exists only at emotional pitches, for only when the spirit
is vibrantly alive is it in a poetic state of being. Because periods
of emotional exaltation cannot be sustained over long spans, the
long poem, as Poe argued, cannot be poetry, certainly not good
poetry. Robinson sympathized with this attitude when he remarked, in reference to the success his long poems were having,
that he was "at a loss to understand how and why so many
people can read over 200 pages of blank verse—I have even
walked by "Paradise Lost" without missing a train." [7] To be

interesting as a whole and not just in isolated parts, a long poem has to rely upon a different appeal than the lyric does; it must engage the intellect, and to do that it has to arouse emotions associated with and satisfied by a comprehensive vision of order. A great deal of intellectual scaffolding is usually necessary to engross the mind in tracing out that order's sources and intricacies, as in Dante's *Divine Comedy* or Milton's *Paradise Lost,* so that truth, not intense passion or sensory delight, is perforce the basis of its success as well as its coherence.

Robinson fully recognized that a poem must give pleasure to merit consideration, but at the same time his primary concern as a poet was truth. And in this latter respect the late long poems are quite successful, even though their comprehensive vision of order entails a minimum of intellectual scaffolding, at least of the traditional sort. Robinson's aversion to systematic thought, to rational categories and relations, as found in Emerson and American thought deriving from him, makes his long poems less amenable to systematic philosophical analysis and less rewarding of the pleasure that comes from contemplating a tightly constructed system. Nevertheless, the poems are deeply rooted in, soundly based upon, and firmly held together by the vision of reality William James called radical empiricism, and thus they do offer the intellectual pleasure of seeing life clearly and seeing it whole. Their justification for being read is that they embody a large, coherent, and fully realized truth.

For that truth to be fully accessible, it must be recognized that, though each emphasizes a different aspect of it, they all treat the same subject; they are all devoted to rendering the truth of the self, so all of them together tell the complete story. Instead of a progress of thought from one to the next, they are concentered, each supplementing the other so that together they constitute a full exploration of the order, or, more exactly, process, that they are intended to articulate. What Robinson said of *Merlin,* that it "was written in anticipation of L. and G. [*Lancelot*], to complement its various incompletenesses, and the two should be read together," [8] is also true for the late long poems from *Roman Bartholow* to *King Jasper.* Though not

101

deliberately written in anticipation of one another, they in fact were and must be read together as a group to understand the whole truth as Robinson finally understood it.

All the late long poems are devoted to tracing their protagonists' passage through spiritual death to rebirth or reawakening; each protagonist loses his "Me" to find the "I," and in doing so passes through disintegration to a higher integration. Roman Bartholow and Matthias achieve freedom through enlightenment; Fernando Nash is reborn through a mystical experience; Cavender, racked by guilt, and Talifer, misled by the seductive beauty of a woman, both win peace; and Fargo, Malory, and King Jasper are saved from themselves through the sacrifice of their personal aspirations to superpersonal considerations. Each discovers the hard way that

> . . . man, even if divine, is mechanism
> While he is here, and so is not himself
> If much of him be broken.   [1012]

Actually, man is mechanism only if broken, only if the diverse aspects of his being are at war with one another, for each protagonist discovers a possibility beyond being broken and thus being a mechanism. Each of them learns through experience that

> Before you build a tower that will remain
> Where it is built and will not crumble down
> To another poor ruin of self, you must be born.
> [1138]

Consequently, the late long poems relate not a partial or abortive, but a completed, action in which a man moves beyond the antagonism between the "I" and the "Me" to a higher ground of freedom and peace through self-knowledge and self-realization.

This higher integration, it must be noted, does not mean a literal reconciliation of self and society, whose estrangement is and must remain a necessary condition of life; rather, it makes possible a union in which the self becomes reconciled to its own being, or its necessity, as Robinson calls it, on a level beyond its relation to society. The objective alienation of self from society is translated into a subjective tension between the "I" and the

"Me," and once the conflict is internalized, the self can become master in its own house. While Robinson's development from "Credo" to "The Man Against the Sky" was made possible by his objectification of the self, just the reverse process was necessary in the long poems and the new "thought" they represent: what existed previously in the world or between man and the world is now assimilated into the self.

For Robinson to tell the truth about it, the self, it would seem, must be a determinable quantity, but he tacitly acknowledged what George Herbert Mead explicitly argued,[9] that the "I" is indeterminable. In one sense it is: the "I" is not a thing and therefore it cannot be defined by its formal properties. But in another sense it can be defined: regarded as a power rather than a thing, it can be identified by what it does. Electricity, for example, is defined as "an agency producing various physical phenomena, as attraction and repulsion, luminous and heating effects, shock to the body, chemical decomposition, etc." [10] Like electricity, the self can be defined functionally, as an agency revealed in various phenomena. So the truth Robinson tells about the self resides in the plot which I have already briefly described and its progress through death to rebirth. And since the climactic experience in what happens to it is a moment of self-discovery and self-realization, the main key to that truth lies in rebirth, typically represented by a passage near the close of *Amaranth:*

> The world around him flamed amazingly
> With light that comforted and startled him
> With joy, and with ineffable release.
> There was a picture of unrolling moments
> In a full morning light, and out of it
> Familiar walls and windows were emerging
> From an inscrutable white mist that melted
> Transparently to air. . . . . . [1392]
> . . . .
> Fargo, partly awake, with eyes half open,
> Saw sunlight and deliverance, and all through him
> Felt a slow gratitude that he was hearing
> Outside, somewhere, at last, the sound of living—
> [1393]

103

What happens to the self comes to a culmination in this moment of deliverance and joy, this return to the world and life, but that moment is linked to, and explained by, a chain of events leading up to it.

The initial state in the self's journey is, of course, the opposite of this climactic one—an imprisonment in blindness and agony. Put another way, it suffers, in A. N. Whitehead's phrase, from an error in "misplaced concreteness" in which the "Me" is mistaken for the real thing, the "I." Amaranth describes this condition to Fargo, in commenting on some damned souls:

> These are men so disordered and wrong sighted,
> So blind with self, that freedom, when they have it,
> Is only a new road, and not a long one,
> To new imprisonment.   [1337]

Here, and on every other occasion he uses the term, Robinson means by "self" the "Me"—egotism, vanity, self-interest, dominance: all those attitudes by which men relate themselves invidiously to other men or arrogate to themselves an exalted status in society or the universe. His terms for the "I," on the other hand, are Power, Will, and Light; viewing it as a philosophical or religious rather than a psychological or sociological matter, Robinson regards the "I" as transcending individual consciousness. Matthias, of *Matthias at the Door,* is a prime example of a man blind with self, in Robinson's sense of the term, or with "Me":

> He was apart,
> Because, being who he was, and as he was,
> His natural station would inevitably
> Be somewhat on an imminence, like his house.
> [1077]
>
> . . . .
> He was not one
> To move unenvied or to fade unseen,
> Or to be elbowed and anonymous
> In a known multitude. There was that in him
> That was not theirs; and that was all of him
> There was for them to know.   [1081]

This is social pride, the assumption of superiority over other men because one has been successful in acquiring wealth and position. Matthias' vanity leads to even greater presumption, however:

> for Matthias pride was more than life.
> So, on a chilly Sunday afternoon,
> Alone there with a winter-laden wind
> Whirling dead leaves over a darkening floor,
> Matthias heard their message and was proud
> That he could meet with patience and high scorn
> A life without a scheme and to no purpose—
> An accident of nameless energies,
> Of which he was a part, and no small part.
> His blindness to his insignificance
> Was like another faith, and would not die. [1127]

This is intellectual pride, the demand that the universe honor the claims of the individual for a rationally meaningful life and justify his arrogantly assumed position as the central figure in the scheme of things. This insistence that life be made subservient to man's intellect is an obvious Faustian characteristic; even more obviously Faustian is the desire for dominance, which was King Jasper's blind obsession. When he realized he had been "wrongsighted," he said of himself,

> "Hebron,
> It was for power that I neglected you—
> So selfishly. It was for power, not gold.
> . . . .
> . . . .You could not have known
> My demon of ambition; for in you,
> Hebron, he never dwelt."   [1425]

King Jasper builds what he assumes to be an indestructible tower from which he, like Faust, can be the master of all he surveys, for he, like Matthias, and also Cavender, who was "afraid of time and life" (1005), seeks control over the vicissitudes of fortune and the flux of time.

Others—Fernando Nash, Fargo, Malory—are not so grandly motivated, but because of some form of pride—an

105

artist's exaggerated notion of his talent, jealousy, revenge—
each is blinded by his desire to exalt the "Me." Men who live on
such heights live precariously, and sooner or later they must
fall. For though it is possible to live by error for a time, eventually, at least in a man of any fiber, the "I" demands its wages
and cannot be refused. All of Robinson's major characters in
the late long poems have one virtue in common with Matthias,

> a man who must have light,
> Or darkness that was rest and certainty,
> With no fool-fire of an unfuelled faith
> Invading it and losing its own spark . . .   [1144]

They are truth seekers, and in their uncompromising demand
for truth lies their dignity. But the truth cannot be sought out,
run down, and captured; like grace, it must come silently out of
the darkness as a gift from an inexplicable source. Once caught
in the vicious circle of pride, a man cannot will that he be
reborn to truth, since in his error he is not even conscious of the
possibility. So spiritual awakening must come to him against his
better judgment through a degeneration and disintegration
wrought by forces external to his self-consciousness. The "Me"
must be sufficiently weakened so that a counterforce can emerge
and abet its total collapse. This is precisely what happens to
King Jasper, who feels the "touch of hidden fingers everywhere"
(1397) on the foundations of his kingdom and life. Identifying
the source of the destructive power, Robinson wrote,

> The fears he felt
> Were not the tinglings of inveiglement;
> They were unsought, inept awakenings
> Of truth he long had fancied was asleep,
> Knowing truth never sleeps.   [1412]

The external force working against his "Me," though sometimes
abetted by circumstances or an empowered person, is strictly
speaking part of King Jasper's own being that he has denied.
Repression was clamped upon the "I" so that self-exaltation
could proceed unhampered; but truth will out, as the saying
goes, and in time the truth seeker's spiritual being revolts

106

against the dominion of the "Me" and adamantly demands that justice be done.

Built into a man is an inexpungable self-corrective principle, a truth that cannot be betrayed with impunity, even though the punishment may not be immediately administered. The nature of this principle and punishment is obliquely revealed by Hebron, the man King Jasper destroyed in order to acquire his kingdom and power, when he says to the latter:

> Did you know what it was that you were doing
> While you enlarged your dream, and swelled and changed,
> Till you were more a monster than a man?
> When I was gone, men said you were a king;
> But you were more. You were almost a kingdom;
> And you forgot that kingdoms are not men.
> They are composite and obscure creations
> Of men, and in a manner are comparable
> To moving and unmanageable machines,
> And somehow are infernally animated
> With a self-interest so omnivorous
> That ultimately they must eat themselves.
> You cannot eat yourself very long and live,
> Jasper; and that's about what you were doing . . .
>   [1425-1426]

Although Hebron makes a severe judgment on the nature of society here, the main thrust of his criticism is aimed at King Jasper, who has become a monster through identifying himself with a kingdom. He and his kingdom being one and the same, what is true of it is also true of him; he, too, is an "unmanageable machine" and "infernally animated," a mechanical and diabolical monster rather than a man. To live blindly, to mistake the "Me" for the "I," is to betray the vital spiritual center, the source of one's humanity, and when this center is betrayed all that remains is a mechanism capable of negation—of self-destruction and the destruction of others. Malory, bent on revenge, the destruction of another person for solace to his pride, degenerates to this extreme state, and there is

> nothing left
> Of [him] but some primitive wheels and springs,
> Wound still to go till he was tired of them,
> And of their ticking.   [1018]

To gain a "Me," especially one of great worth, it is necessary to lose one's soul, because what exalts the "Me" in the struggle for superiority automatically denigrates the "I." The inevitable wages of pride are self-alienation, a kind of death in which a man, though physically alive, of necessity kills all that he touches, including himself. Under such circumstances a man is a "nay-sayer" whose thought and action negate himself, truth, and reality.

All the protagonists in the late long poems are victims of self-alienation, doomed on a death-bound course to self-ruin. All become "players to our necessities" (777) when pride becomes more important to them than life. They all inevitably come, like Matthias, to the door of death, which takes many forms but in every case is the ultimate negation and bitterest agony. Here is Fernando Nash's visit to that door in a hallucination:

> And still the music sounded, weird but firm,
> And the more fearful as it forged along
> To a dark and surging climax, which at length
> Broke horribly into coarse and unclean laughter
> That rose above a groaning of the damned;
> And through it all there were those drums of death,
> Which always had been haunting him from childhood.
> . . . .
> . . . . the rats
> Danced madly to the long cacophony
> They made, and they made faces at Fernando
> The while they danced—till one of them, the leader,
> Bowed mockingly, and vanished through the keyhole,
> As he had come; and after him went others,
> Each with a leering courtesy as he went . . .   [940]

To die spiritually is to discover that all that one has been or aspired to be, the "Me," in short, is nothing, is, in fact, a horrible mockery of the true and the good. And when that discovery occurs, life becomes meaningless and intolerable.

Those who have engaged in a "mischosen warfare against self and nature" (1349) cannot take off the "armor of negation" (943) they don at this point and so pass through the door by suicide. Others—the truth seekers, with their unquenchable spark of life and affirmation—consume that armor in the fire of the "I's" passion to be reborn out of the "Me's" ruins. Fernando Nash is among these, and as he reawakened to life,

> He was hungry—
> Hungry beyond a longer forced endurance,
> But in this new unwillingness not to live,
> No longer forced, there was a gratefulness
> Of infinite freedom and humility,
> After a bondage of indignant years
> And evil sloth; and there was in this calm,
> Which had unlooked for been so long in coming,
> A balanced wealth of debts and benefits
> Vaster than all ambition or achievement.
> Hereafter it would be enough to serve,
> And let the chosen shine.   [944]

With the death of the "Me" and the rebirth of the "I" he understands, like Malory, that

> There was time
> For living in himself and on himself,
> Like a thought-eating worm, and dying of it
> Unthought of, or for life larger than that,
> Larger than self, and one that was not death. [1065]

It is then that he hears "outside, somewhere, at last, the sound of living" (1392) and is free to live again, to live for good rather than evil.

As pride gives way to selflessness, the protagonist becomes conscious of something outside of or beyond the "Me." Every protagonist in the late long poems consciously or unconsciously asks of himself, as Penn-Raven asks of Roman Bartholow, if

> we see beyond ourselves
> Nothing, what have we within ourselves
> Worth seeing or worth saving?   [824]

And they learn that the answer to the question is,

> you are to serve
> Henceforth as one may serve who is alive
> Among so many that are not alive. [829]

109

Or as it was said of the prideful Matthias,

> he must be born,
> And then must live; and he who had been always
> So promptly served, and was to be a servant,
> Must now be of some use in a new world . . .
>
> [1154]

The truth that never sleeps awakens the protagonist to the knowledge that life is greater than pride. So to be reborn is to discover, contrary to one's conscious knowledge and desire, that once the "Me" yields hegemony to the "I" life is supremely valuable. Malory, like the others, experienced this rebirth, and as he watched the ocean he saw that

> Those flashing waves were life; they were not death,
> Or sleep. The power that made them flash was power,
> It was not nothing. It was like a wish
> To live, and an awakening wish to serve.   [1060]

Deliverance and joy come when, freed from the prison of the "Me," the individual subordinates himself to a "cause" that transcends his egocentric motives.

But again the discovery is not literally of something outside man. Fernando Nash, for instance, commented on his rebirth by saying, "And fear not for my soul. I have found that, / Though I have lost all else" (953). Where he found a soul, Young Gideon found a man:

> Now that he knew the man that in himself
> Had been a stranger, freedom, like a bell,
> Sang through him . . .   [1208-1209]

Both, however, make the same discovery, of man's innermost being, of the man within the man, as St. Paul spoke of it. They learn that the "Me" is an illusion born of pride, and that reality, the "I," is greater than a man's idea of himself or his social identity. Like Malory, they come to realize that

> If I had learned,
> In time, to know that I was not the law
> That made me live, I should have done more shining,
> And in a light more grateful to my eyes.   [1049]

They first recognize that there is a law which begets and sustains them, and then they subordinate the "Me" to the "I" by placing it in service to that law. That law, therefore, despite the associations of the word with moral commandments or regulatory powers, is not outside man but is his own being.

The deliverance of the man within the man is the moment of self-discovery and self-realization, for as the "Me" dies so that the "I" can be reborn, the truth seeker's illusions fall from his eyes and he sees for the first time what truly is. Until then he has sought to build a life on something outside himself or on external relations, not on the truth of his own being. But at deliverance he knows that authentic existence is only achieved through conforming the soul to its own reality. To accomplish this he must integrate his conscious faculties with the ground of their being, placing them in service to that ground so that he can become an agent for the affirmation and enhancement of life. Rebirth is the achievement, or reachievement, of a free and integrated spirit through a return to the inherently moral "I" as the source of one's motives and values. The dualism of thought and will, Robinson recognized, is not resolved through one's becoming a stone, but through a moral-spiritual enlightenment, achieved through suffering, in which man's powerful propensity toward egotism is sacrificed before the law that makes life possible.

The indeterminable true self, the "I," has the two determinable qualities, both manifested most obviously during death-rebirth, of moral integrity and the need for truth. If this were all that composes the "I," Robinson would have found it easily definable, but a third quality, most obvious after rebirth, eliminates any possibility of formal definition. That quality is freedom. Robinson knew that materialism negates freedom and thus negates spirit, so that a repudiation of materialism and an affirmation of man required, above all, the affirmation of freedom. Paradoxically, freedom for the protagonists in the late long poems results from yielding to necessity, an apparent bondage; but it is no paradox really, for, when one is reborn, freedom is simply an inherent part of one's being. As Roman

111

Bartholow learned, once enlightened, his "doom is to be free" (825), there being no choice in the matter.

Of course, the question Robinson had to confront at this point was, free of what, for what? The answer, though implicit in all the long poems and much of the journey toward truth already discussed, is most fully given in *Roman Bartholow,* in which Roman is already enlightened at the outset; at the beginning of the poem, for instance, it is said of him, "He looked about him with a life renewed / Upon a world renewed" (835). The poem, therefore, traces Roman's education in what it means to be free. He learns, first of all, like every protagonist of the late long poems, that pride is less than life, that freedom entails an escape from the bondage of the "Me"; he also learns that "tradition is less than life" (770), that freedom requires escape from bondage to the past, whether the past be represented by custom or learning; and he also learns that freedom means loneliness, inescapable estrangement from the external supports of other persons or social life, the courage to go it alone. Other protagonists may be added to this list; Talifer learns, for example, that freedom requires antirationalism, or repudiation of the abstract for the concrete; and King Jasper learns that it requires a disbelief in the permanence of any social order. But all this education makes up one large truth: to be truly alive is to be free of everything that hinders life from being true to itself. Roman Bartholow jettisons everything extraneous until all he has left is the pure impulse to live; and shorn of all accidental accretions, free of every restrictive element, life and the self are simply an "uncertain fire" (944), a mysterious energy with the capacity as well as the desire to assert and perpetuate its existence.

Cavender was rebuked by the apparition of his murdered wife for being afraid of life and time. But all the other protagonists are equally guilty before they are reborn. Rebirth for them begets a confident, tranquil dedication to life, and that means a confident, tranquil acceptance of time, for self in addition to being free exists in time—indeed, to be free it must exist in time. Flax, in *Amaranth,* advises another,

> Be at peace
> With time; for in this region where we are,
> There is no other peace.   [1345]

Reality is flux, change, process; this is a crucial truth in the
protagonist's education in freedom, learned most frequently
through painful experience. Some, in fact, cannot tolerate that
truth—for example, Honoria, King Jasper's wife, who "was not
made for changes" (1474) and so commits suicide. But the
truth seekers come to know through failure that all forms of
apparent certainty or security—honor, achievement, possession, dominance, tradition, the status quo, etc.—being contrary
to the nature of things, "ultimately . . . must eat themselves"
(1426) in the desperation of defending themselves against
change. Zoe, King Jasper's nemesis and representative of truth,

> is too free and holy,
> Or so he [Jasper's son] says, to let herself be bound
> Or tangled in the flimsy nets or threads
> Of church or state . . . .
> . . . . she seems to be a sort
> Of charming and transfigured wasp, equipped
> To sting the mightiest spiders of convention
> And fly away from them as free as ever.   [1402]

Time cannot be stopped, life cannot be compressed into permanent molds, and if either is tried, an inevitable explosion is the
consequence.

Conversely, and perhaps more significantly, time is inherent in the self. The self is a potential, an aspiration, a power,
that genuinely exists only in action. Since action is movement
out of the past through the present into the future, time is an
essential attribute. But mere progress through time, which can
be mechanical, is not enough for the self; its action must be
creative; life must be purposive and result in the extension and
enhancement of itself. Consequently, the self can never rest on
its achievements, its past being nothing more than a souvenir,
but must continually act, must continually assert and reaffirm
its existence. To be, it must eternally renew its existence
through creative action, because to act is to be alive, and to be

113

alive is to act. Moreover, it is impossible to be alive and not to act. Acting entails purpose, which entails choice, which in turn entails morality. Morality presupposes freedom, which presupposes power, and both presuppose time. To be true to itself, the self must be all these things, the necessary conditions of its existence, but finally and simply, the irreducible truth about the self is that it acts. For this reason, the past, which is gone, and the present, which is going, are less important for the self than the future, which is an open territory of possibility. For it, what is becomes secondary to what can be.

The "I," the man within the man, equated with the law that makes man live, is the power to be and to act. The self, Robinson therefore came to understand, is not identified with character or personality, with, that is, the conscious, social aspects of man's being, but is an activity, a truth-demanding, moral, creative force not identifiable with or derivable from a role, idea, institution, community, state, or culture. The true self is not a phenomenon but the begetter and sustainer of phenomena, the energy behind the mask of things, the ground of their existence, the power for transformation and transcendence of the presently achieved. When Robinson comes to view man as a creature for whom the "I" is his essential being, it follows, as Charles Cestre, Robinson's endorsed interpreter, detected, that he believes that "there is no such thing as one permanent ego, but . . . we pass successively through various personalities, as we go through various phases of experience." [11] In this he anticipated Existentialism, which claims, in the words of Everett W. Knight, that "there is no self considered as a sort of 'thing'; it is an intention, a direction, an orientation." [12] In the end, for Robinson, too, the self is an intention, a "structure of action," which knows itself and the world through doing and making; an artificer in time and space building towers as monuments to the primal energy that truly knows itself only when the power for production is given priority over the product.

But Robinson did not become the naive child he had rejected. He understood that man is obviously not absolutely free to do or make anything he pleases. He not only has to act

within the physical limitations of time and space, which include
history as well as contemporary circumstances, but he cannot
will that he physically become, for example, a serpent or God,
though he may attempt to emulate one or the other morally.
Robinson, fully cognizant of this matter, took account of it by
stating that "There is no cure for self; / There's only an occa-
sional revelation" (1137). Here, as always, he uses "self" to
mean the "Me," and his point is that as a creature of this world
a man acts from a given place, at a definite time, with finite
knowlege and finite power. For him, a reborn man is still a man,
not God; when reborn, he is an agent of spirit, asserting and
extending its existence through acting, not universal, disembodied spirit itself. Moreover, he knew that one is not reborn once
and for all but must continually renew himself; he must con-
stantly transcend his past by regaining and reaffirming his freedom from completed acts and present circumstances. This limitation results in the paradox, applicable to Robinson as well as
his characters, that "In art you must esteem yourself or perish"
(1324). On the surface the source of all evil, a healthy pride
ultimately begets good, for without it, the spirit dies; without
valuing what one is, without moral self-acceptance, without
self-love, there can be no passion to live. Robinson himself as
well as his heroes or truth seekers had to possess the talent,
confidence, and courage to venture beyond the norms of previously charted and institutionalized experience. His place in
the rhythm of things required that he experience the extremes,
that he have "the courage to be" outside of conventional boundaries and supports, because his special task as poet was to keep
the established order from too fully realizing its tendency to
solidify through reminding it of its spiritual sources and periodi-
cally injecting new shots of "soul" into its lethargic "mind."
Thus the pride that doomed Matthias to a fall saved him to live
again and Robinson to write truly original poetry .

Though reconciled in rebirth, the dualism of the "I" and
"Me," as Robinson saw it, is not permanently annihilated. Like
Emerson before him, he recognized that "human life is made up
of two elements, power and form, and the proportions must be

invariably kept if we would have it sweet and sound." [13] At the center of the truth Robinson gives utterance to is a clear-sighted understanding that the self is a composite of the "I" and "Me," and the annihilation of either puts an end to life. In order to live or be man, it is necessary, he realized, to cherish the puzzling complexity and ironic dichotomy inherent in every concrete, individual self, for to simplify rather than dynamically balance antitheses is to repudiate vital and human existence. To care for life and man is to repudiate extremes; it is, in Robinson's own words, to "have the spirit of wise moderation and love of classical completeness." [14] The self is a delicate balance of opposites. "All things," Robinson said on this point,

> that are worth having are perilous,
> And have their resident devil, respectively.
> There's this that I have here, there's love, pride, art,
> Humility, ambition, power and glory,
> The kingdom itself, which may come out all right,
> And truth. They are all very perilous,
> And admirable, so long as there is in them
> Passion that knows itself.   [1131]

This knowledge is of course self-knowledge, consciousness of the existential relation between the personal and spiritual or the ego and the other, not intellectual comprehension of the ultimate nature of the universe. During rebirth Matthias is told by a voice from beyond the grave, in answer to his question about the meaning of life,

> If you could know, Matthias, you would be free.
> But you are far from knowing, and are not free . . .
>   [1151]

This kind of knowledge is intellectual understanding of absolutes; this kind of freedom is complete control over life. Neither is possible for the self. Awaking in midstream, with life flowing through and about it, carried ceaselessly by a current without detectable shores or ascertainable direction, as long as the self is a creature in this world it is life's servant, like it or not. Grimly acknowledging the human predicament, Zoe remarks,

> I don't say what God is, but it's a name
> That somehow answers us when we are driven
> To feel and think how little we have to do
> With what we are.   [1472]

However, what man can achieve, despite the limitations of his knowledge and power, is wisdom. The self's supreme truth is its power to know most importantly the immediacy of its interior life and outer circumstances, the existential facts of its existence; and knowing and accepting this, it can achieve such a relation between the mind and the soul that life will flow from the heart of its being, the "I," and it will live true to itself.

The world as an aesthetic phenomenon

It is the office, I doubt not, of this age
to annul that adulterous divorce which
superstition of many ages has effected
between the intellect and holiness.

Ralph Waldo Emerson

Esthetic cannot be sharply marked off
from intellectual experience since the
latter must bear an esthetic stamp to
be itself complete.

John Dewey

A work of art is an abstract or epitome
of the world. It is the result or expression of nature, in miniature.

Ralph Waldo Emerson

We have seen what happens to the self in its journey to
enlightenment according to the late long poems, but what the
self specifically is at any given moment depends upon what it
does with its freedom and creative power. In Robinson's case,
that was to make poems. Robinson's poetry is therefore the

118

product of his "I's" activity, so that what is true for Robinson's self is also true for his poetry. His poetry, for instance, has its dual aspects of language and reality, or letter and spirit; though fashioned by the "Me," it is ultimately the result of liberated and liberating power originating in his "I."

On occasion Robinson would disclaim any knowledge of what poetry is, but when disposed to be more assertive, he would say, as he caused Rembrandt to remark, "I am but a living instrument / Played upon by powers that are invisible" (589). Such a statement is not much more definite than a profession of ignorance, but it is as far as Robinson could go simply because it is as much as he could ascertain. Speaking directly for himself, he could be no more specific: "I discovered long ago," he said, "that an artist is just a sort of living whistle through which Something blows." [1] A poet compulsively serves a transpersonal power which uses him and his productions to exercise and affirm its being while he remains in ignorance of its ultimate nature and purposes. His existence, talent, and inspiration are not his possessions; instead, he belongs to them, serving as an agent for their expression. Although employing inappropriate mechanical imagery, Hermann Hagedorn provides the fullest account of this, Robinson's final conception of poetry, in his statement that Robinson

had a mystic sense of his calling. At bottom, he did not think of his poetry as his own achievement. He fetched it from subterranean streams deeper than any driven cogitation of his. He was not its creator, he knew, but only the pump which brought it to the surface, an instrument of transmission whom the power he had a way of denoting "Whatever-it-is" had chosen to use. . . . He himself could do nothing about it all, except to keep the instrument clean and clear.[2]

Obviously, this is also Robinson's understanding of the self. On the whole Robinson's definition of poetry is rather vague, yet this much about it is specific: the power, Whatever-it-is, is Something—with capital letters—which is quite different from nothing, and that Something plays, blows, and uses—in short, acts. An indeterminable, transpersonal power, clearly not mechanical or electrical energy, is the source of a poet's ultimate being and therefore of a poem, too.

This conception of reality as power is characteristic of the new thought in the last decades of the nineteenth century. George Santayana, for example, set out to determine the irreducible elements of existence, and discovered

that at once, by a mere act of self-examination and frankness, the spirit has come upon one of the most important and radical of religious perceptions. It has perceived that though it is living, it is powerless to live; that though it may die, it is powerless to die; and that altogether, at every moment and in every particular, it is in the hands of some alien and inscrutable power.[3]

For materialism and literary naturalism this power becomes the great leveler, with the result that, as Frank Norris put it, "Men were naught, death was naught, life was naught; Force only existed—Force that brought men into the world . . . Force that made the wheat grow. . . ."[4] But Robinson and his *avant-garde* contemporaries did not see it that way. True, in their new world, change, process, continuous birth and death hold unchallengeable dominion over everything, but that does not necessarily eliminate truth and value. A creature such as man, having a teleological disposition and doomed to act, must morally justify and intellectually affirm his existence. If he continues to live, he implicitly affirms at least life, if nothing more specific. Understanding this, Robinson could not tolerate a permanent estrangement of will and belief, and so he humanized power— that is, he interpreted reality so as to allow for, rather than negate, man's will to live.

Robinson had a choice between two different kinds of power. One kind, though its effects may be to propel, change the state, construct, or disintegrate, was a mechanical agency of causality or of quantitative, determined relations. The other kind acts through a body, being expressed and directed by it, in which case it is creative, a resource by which an entity enhances itself or evolves into a higher form. This latter kind necessarily entails qualitative change: it is the power by which aspiration toward greater life gets transformed into action, not a system of energy in which output equals input. The first was the assumption supporting mechanism, the second the assumption supporting the theory of evolution, so that both were living options for Robinson. He obviously rejected the first, which is perhaps appropriate to matter but clearly antithetical to life. That leaves the second, but though he chose it, he was not in sympathy with the prevailing theory of evolution; it could not satisfactorily account for the life of the imagination. In fact, though early in his career he spoke as though the theory might be valid, later he dismissed it outright, the disjunction he insisted upon between man and nature apparently ruling out the possibility of natural phenomena evolving into spiritual being. Though the Something is a transpersonal power, Robinson did not associate it with the development of the species or historical progress, nor with a world spirit, Hegelian or otherwise, which uses men as means to work out its destiny. Actually, for Robinson an entity cannot evolve into what it is not but can become only what it truly is. His realism imposed its boundaries upon his idea of power, and, therefore, on his sense of what a poem can be and do. His attitude is classical and Christian: power acts through a body but only for self-realization in an individual; it is not a grand march through time but a pulsating creation and destruction, not the implacable drive of history toward a millennium but moral awareness here and now. Thus he could say, while making time an inherent condition of this world, that he didn't believe in time; the Something and the "I" are simply eternal activity that perpetually exists for the sake of existence. The world is not evolving toward a higher state and eventual perfection, and since it is not, poetry is not able to play a role in helping it overcome what it now is.

Charles Cestre correctly identified Robinson's idea of power when he said, "In this Robinson is modern, and he is American; for it is in America, if anywhere, that the Life-Force—energy, will-to-live, desire for action—makes itself heard." [5] Robinson is modern but not just American; his conception of life as force aligns him with William James, Bergson,

Whitehead, Shaw, Nietzsche, and Unamuno, his contemporaries who celebrated life with notions of plurality, the adventure of ideas, the *élan vital,* the Life-Force, the will to power. Although Robinson tends to be cautious and solemn where these men are vigorously assertive and confident, nevertheless he accepted the will to live as the fundamental fact of man's existence. Like most of these men, he ignores all theories envisaging history, life, and society as governed by transpersonal values, or that favor an abstraction over the concrete person. For him, life does not exist in the abstract, only in single, separate, concrete entities, and the highest attainment of "Whatever-it-is," at least from man's point of view, is consciousness, which appears only in separate persons, so that its supreme achievement is individuality. There is no larger design of which we can have knowledge. Robinson, in fact, is even more modern than Cestre thought; he is close to Existentialism in that he repudiates the historical and sociological views of force in favor of a view that locates the power in the will and imagination of the individual. Man is not made by and for larger cosmic designs but makes himself in the sense that the aspirations of the power begin and end in his need for individual moral action. If "Existentialism is a humanism," giving autonomy and the highest value to the individual person, Robinson's poetry is humanistic too, for in it the individual exists as an end in himself; the transpersonal power and the individual exist in and through each other and simultaneously affirm the existence of each other in enlightened acts.

In espousing a humanistic idea of power, Robinson rejected the dominant motive in modern Western culture, the Faustian, Baconian, scientific drive for power over nature through knowledge. He is not concerned with the will to power, but with the will to live, and the will to live is not self-assertion through the use, manipulation, or alteration of nature, man, or oneself. Rather, it is obedience to the mysterious law that makes man live, that is his origin and sustenance, and that endows him with the capacities for truth, moral awareness, and creativity. The power, a caldron of energy for the most part accurately represented by the dynamo, becomes in Robinson's eyes capable of consciousness and creative action in one of its states of activity. Therefore, the Something does not reduce man and life to naught but, on the contrary, makes them possible—indeed, creates and thus proclaims their value. Provided man keeps the self "clean and clear," the Something can flow through him, and if he is a poet, it will bear fruit in authentic poems.

Obviously, true poems, according to Robinson's view, cannot be didactic statements about the spirit. Rather than being a statement about the best in man, they are the best in him, an expression of his highest capability of awareness and activity, the spirit flowing into the world. Consequently, whether an assertion of the spirit's predicament when imprisoned or of its truth when free, a poem is simply the manifestation and affirmation of spirit, the power that makes the poem possible. Robinson, once free of inherited notions, came to understand consciously that a poem does not mean but simply is; it does not represent but presents; it is not a symbol remotely standing for something beyond itself; nor is it a self-contained structure of words or a fiction. When his mind became sufficiently integrated with his soul, he knew that a poem was nothing more nor less than a sign announcing the presence and power of Something.

But it is not pure spirit; it is the Something incarnate. A poem has its "Me" and its "I," its letter and its spirit, its social form and role and its mystical reality. It is an artifice of words, whereas poetry, the "spirit" of the poem, equivalent to the "I," is the creative power which begot and inhabits the poem. It is possible, for instance, to read "Flammonde" as a poem on poetry in which the mind attempts to comprehend the poetic power. Read this way, it testifies to its own being as a composite of finite form and infinite power.

In a world in which reality is power and all existence interminably changes, Robinson could readily have fallen into despair for want of certainty and rest. But though his life may have seemed blind and futile at one time, he was able to believe in its darkest moments that his existence was an expression of Something and that in a proper state of mind he could serve and enjoy it. Recognizing this, he knew that regardless of how ephemeral his creations might be, as he was made, so he is a maker. Emerson saw this quite clearly:

Every spirit builds itself a house, and beyond its house a world, and beyond its world a heaven. Know then that the world exists for you. For you is the phenomenon perfect. What we are, that only can we see. All that Adam had, all that Caesar could, you have and can do. Adam called his house, heaven and earth; Caesar called his house, Rome; you perhaps call yours a cobbler's trade; a hundred acres of plowed land; or a scholar's garret. Yet life for life and point for point your dominion is as great as theirs, though without fine names. Build therefore your own world. As fast as you conform your life to the pure idea in your mind, that will unfold its great proportions.[6]

Following in Emerson's footsteps, Robinson built his spirit's house—or tower, to use the image he preferred in his last period—out of poems, finishing it off with the late long poems, in which the mind, acknowledging the hegemony of the "I" over the "Me," serves the soul in order to utter its truth and thereby arrive at a spiritual realization of things and their significance. By living his vocation through to the realization of its inner truth, he learned that the meaning of life is in the making of it, or just in making, since life is perpetual re-creation of the true and the good. As Timberlake, a character in *Matthias at the Door,* remarks,

> We don't increase ourselves with our regrets
> Unless there's action in them. Let us act. [1130]

Robinson acted by writing poems, and though he acknowledged the validity of other modes of life, it was through his writing that he increased himself and conformed his life to the pure idea in his soul. The poems were his means, in the language of radical empiricism, of enlarging consciousness and therefore life; for if, as Robinson and his fellow contemporaries assumed, being more fully aware is equivalent to being more fully alive, then his poetry as a whole charts his progress into fuller life.

Though Robinson's poetry is dedicated to, and succeeds in, defining itself, he did not deliberately work toward or consciously hold a systematic theory of poetry. An antitheorist, he

124

vigorously insisted that he did not, as when he wrote to Amy Lowell, "I have absolutely no theories. I don't care a pin-feather what form a poem is written in so long as it makes me sit up. 'Imagist' work, per se, taken as a theory apart from one special form, seems to be rather too self-conscious and exclusive to stand the test of time." [7] He did not conceive of poetry abstractly; instead, he lived it as his calling. In living it, without necessarily intending to, of course, he participated in the profound change Whitehead said was taking place in Western civilization and affecting "every department of thought." He was a revolutionary, in effect, and in his department he did his share to inaugurate the reign of art in a realm once ruled by reason.

Empiricism ruled the day, and certainly poetry did not escape the stress empiricism placed on sight at any time during Robinson's career. Indeed, it forced decisive innovations in style and technique. These innovations begin to appear in the poetry of Robinson and Frost, who used the colloquial diction of everyday, concrete language; local characters and color, actual people in an actual time and place; and realistic motifs about contemporary social events and issues. Later poetry, however, such as Imagistic poetry with its free verse and images, and T. S. Eliot's with its image associationism, allusions, symbols, and myth, more vividly shows the great pressure empiricism was exerting. Amy Lowell recorded its impact when she proclaimed: "Externality, the Imagist and modern attitude, cuts the poet away from introspection and focuses his attention on the object as interesting in itself." [8] And Ezra Pound, with a different emphasis, also recorded that impact when he listed as his first principle, "To paint the thing as I see it." [9]

Though a complex phenomenon, Imagism derived most of its impetus from the desire of poets to emulate science. Pound's call to "make it new" was, among other things, an insistence that poetry base itself upon the assumptions and ideals of scientific empiricism. To be sure, Imagism represents the extreme influence of empiricism on poetry. But under its influence the mainstream of modern poetry became almost exclusively concerned with "sensate experience, with sight and sound, the

125

immediate feel of things." [10] If taken literally and strictly, not just as the commonplace that art works its effects through the senses, this concern leads to a poetry that, parallel to radical empiricism in philosophy, "dissolves thought and structure in feeling and sensory perception." [11] Actually, Yvor Winters, a defender of "reason" and an unrelenting critic of empiricism in poetry, used this phrase to condemn Eliot and Pound, and through them all of modern poetry that is related to theirs by common preconceptions. One may not agree with his judgment, but the accuracy of his observation is unquestionable.

But Winters, it must be noted, speaks of sensory perception and feeling, not simply of sight. The role sight played at the time Robinson was writing can be misleading if empiricism is conceived too narrowly. It must be understood in literature as well as in philosophy as a return to the concrete which embraced both scientific and radical empiricism, or included both sense and sensibility. When empiricism is understood in this inclusive sense, Imagist poetry and T. S. Eliot's have a common base; both assume that reality is immediately experienced. To render the immediately experienced, Imagism, with a strong affinity for science and sense, emphasized externality, subordinating, indeed almost excluding, human passion and will from poetry; whereas Eliot's poetry, symbolic in style and favoring sensibility, makes these the essential elements in experience. The former focuses upon natural objects, that which is supposedly separate from and independent of man's consciousness; [12] the latter concentrates on inner being, using symbols or objective correlatives to reveal the reality directly perceived in experience. Despite this difference, both subscribe to the same basic epistemological principle and both, therefore, are an empirical or "sensate" [13] poetry.

Beginning with the Imagists, and paralleling the emergence of the dichotomy of naturalism and subjectivism in modern fiction, modern poetry split into these two distinct types along the lines of scientific and radical empiricism. But Imagism and Symbolistic poetry in America are later stages in the development of a seed planted earlier. Though the plant is more easily identified in its later stages of growth, it is not quite the same entity as the seed. For in the last decades of the nineteenth century the two forms of empiricism existed in conjunction with one another, not compatibly but nevertheless inseparably. Robinson, along with Frost, who criticized Imagism as an attempt to write poetry according to a program derived from scientific empiricism, insisted that poetry's province was man's total response to life. The difference between these poets and Imagism can be seen in a remark about T. E. Hulme, one of the major spokesmen for the movement. "Convinced of man's ineffectiveness as a seer who can reveal the mystery of the universe," Stanley K. Coffman has written, "Hulme insisted that he turn his eyes from searching the horizon to examining a limited area around his feet." [14] Robinson differs from Hulme in his refusal to stop searching the horizon for ultimate meanings. He does not reveal the mystery of the universe, but he does honor it as the poet's essential subject, asserting thereby man's deepest intellectual claim on life. In effect, by refusing to confine himself to examining a limited area about his feet, by refusing to substitute objects for the soul or separate the soul from the world, he claimed as his subject the full spectrum of experience reported by the inner and outer senses, man's total being, while still accepting the empirical limitation to what appears to be. As a consequence he wrote a poetry that stresses sensibility at the same time it does sight. It was a poetry, in Robinson's phrase, of both "observation and experience," or a poetry of radical empiricism. Finding himself as a poet in the same situation James was as a philosopher, he took as his subject consciousness, approached it empirically, and used reflective intellect to make what he could out of it.

Though an antitheorist, Robinson did not "dissolve intellect into feeling and sensory perception"; he did not banish the mind from the world or his poetry. Instead, following the same course science was taking with symbolic logic, non-Euclidean geometry, relativity and nuclear physics, and the theory of evolution, he kept the intellect intimately engaged in curtailing its own powers. In science, assumptions that had stood firm for from two hundred to two thousand years were suddenly untenable or true only within limited contexts. Of even vaster proportions than the Copernican, this intellectual revolution in science dissolved the rock upon which the sciences as well as the humanities and arts stood, so that old credentials were no longer valid, old justifications no longer rang true, in any area of knowledge. Had science not abandoned its materialistic assumptions, the efforts of the humanities and the arts would have struck impotently against the rock of materialism, as they had for the Romantics and the Victorians. With repeated revelations of reason's limits in mathematics and physics, science freed the mind to speculate, to imagine, and to create by destroying the grounds for belief in the commensurability of rational categories with reality. It opened the way for what a twentieth-century architect called "humanity's epochal graduation from the inert, materialistic nineteenth century into the dynamic, abstract twentieth century." [15] But science, it must be remembered, is an intellectual discipline, and so these new ideas and attitudes result from the intellect's intellectually discovering and voluntarily accepting its own limitations in the face of reality. For Robinson, as for science, the mind figures prominently in this anti-intellectual intellectualism, and as the abstract takes on greater significance, its prestige and powers grow.

Once intellect diminishes its authority in the above way, testimony to it from other faculties gains in stature. Confronted with the task of interpreting an "irrational" world, Bergson, Whitehead, and Dewey, for instance, gave epistemological and metaphysical primacy to the aesthetic, and in doing so they implied thereby that art was a more inclusive and incisive mode of knowing, was a closer analogue to reality, than logic. The first two, originally scientists, gave aesthetics its central position in the scheme of things in the course of trying to explain the reality that biology and physics revealed to them. For their purposes they assumed, as F. S. C. Northrop put it, that "the theoretic component presupposes the aesthetic component of experience, in its own verification . . . the aesthetic factor being as primary and hence as justified a criterion of trustworthy knowledge and of the good and divine in culture as is the theoretical component." [16] Yet all these men were philosophers, thinkers trying to make intellectual sense out of what they took to be the essential data about reality. In doing so they put the intellect to work with the imagination, making the two partners rather than competitors, which is exactly what Robinson does with them in his late poetry.

Now it is sometimes argued that poetry, whose domain is values, and science, whose domain is fact, are mortal enemies. Scientific reality and aesthetic reality, some have argued, are diametrically opposed in the modern world. However valid such a notion may be for other times and places or as a historical generalization, it does not apply to Robinson, the above-mentioned philosophers, or the new science. For Whitehead and Bergson, to repeat, science and art complement one another in exploring radically empirical reality. They did not abandon science when they turned to aesthetics but used aesthetic assumptions to explain and advance scientific discoveries.[17] Likewise, William James, also a scientist (a psychologist), though he argued passionately against materialism in defending the will to believe, never questioned the authority of science. His defense of the will to believe quite explicitly gave the will freedom to believe only where science was incapable of certainty. He saw no necessary contradiction between science and radical empiricism; between them they encompassed the disjunctive and conjunctive elements in experience, science taking as its province the former, aesthetics, the latter; the one analytical, the other synthetic.

Nor did Robinson have any quarrel with science as such, only with scientism or specific scientific doctrines. He did write, in *Matthias at the Door:*

> There's more of you for you to find, Matthias,
> Than science has found yet, or may find soon.
> Science that blinds its eyes incessantly
> With a new light that fades and leaves them aching,
> Whatever it sees, will be a long time showing
> To you, Matthias, what you have striven so hard
> To see in the dark. [1150]

Here science is criticized for its limitations and errors, but Robinson does not reject science, only certain scientific ideas—mainly materialism, but evolution to some extent, also. His respect for it, and there is hardly any greater respect, came out in his statement, "There's a non-theological religion on the way, probably to be revealed by science when science comes definitely to the jumping-off place. It is really there now, but isn't quite ready to say so." [18]

In the materialistic dualism Robinson inherited, science and poetry, intellect and imagination, were at odds with one another. "During the nineteenth century," according to Wylie Sypher,

art and science became alienated as they had not been alienated in the enlightenment; thus the intellectual roots of art were cut. Experiments such as impressionism and the naturalistic novel adapted certain methods from science; yet on the whole art and science seemed to be two incompatible kinds of experience or knowledge, and scientific theory and aesthetic theory seemed contrary.[19]

This deep dissociation of man's inner being from the phenomenal world made it necessary for Carlyle, Arnold, and others to defend poetry and the spirit by disengaging them from science. This was not true in America, however. Emerson and Thoreau, for instance, had no complaint against legitimate science and, in fact, put it to good use in their thought. In any event, by the time of Robinson's maturity science and art were reunited, as William Carlos Williams acknowledged by stating that "when Einstein promulgated the theory of relativity he could not have foreseen its moral and intellectual implications. He could not have foreseen for a certainty its influence on the writing of poetry." [20] Characteristic of the new attitude, and stating it in greater detail, is Naum Gabo's remark that

Whatever exists in nature, exists in us in the form of our awareness of its existence. All creative activities of Mankind consist in the search for an expression of that awareness. . . . The artist of today cannot possibly escape the impact science is making on the whole mentality of the human race. . . . The artist's task is not so pragmatic and straightforward as the scientist's; nevertheless, both the

artist and the scientist are prompted by the same creative urge to
find a perceptible image of the hidden forces in nature of which they
are both aware. . . . I do not know of any idea in the history of
man's culture that developed in a separate and independent com-
partment of the human mind. . . . To my mind it is a fallacy to
assume that the aspects of life and nature which contemporary
science is unfolding are only communicable through science
itself. . . .[21]

When this is so, and it was for Robinson, it follows that poetry
and science or intellect work hand in hand to discover and
create truth. There are some real differences between science
and poetry, of course, and they must not be forgotten, but Robinson instinctively knew that intellect provides the forms for
existence, and imagination provides the power; and, like Emerson before him, he was aware that the balance between them
must be kept sweet and sound.

When the hostility between the intellect and imagination
abates, as it did in Robinson's late poems, facts, laws, static
order—the pillars of a world of essences and fixed relations—
give way to freedom, possibility, and power. Evolution, purpose, activity, emerge with new value and new vitality in a
world affording them scope. Not only is the mind free to speculate, imagine, and create, but life—action, that is, as well as
thought—is free, too. Reality is a restless, aspiring energy press-
ing relentlessly forward. Such a reality, needless to say, is a
haven for the poet and poetry; everything that poetry is, everything that it can do, is not simply tolerated but encouraged and
valued because reality is itself an artist, having a persistent urge
to create greater and higher forms of order, realization, and
significance. The Russian philosopher Nicolai Berdyaev went
straight to the heart of this truth, realized so clearly and completely by Robinson in his late poems, that the world is an
aesthetic phenomenon, in *The Meaning of the Creative Act,*
where he wrote:

Artistic creativeness best reveals the meaning of the creative act.
. . . It is even an accepted expression to call the creative element in
all spheres of spiritual activity "artistic." A clearly creative attitude
towards science, social life, philosophy or morals, we consider artis-

131

tic. And even the Creator of the world is considered in the aspect of the great artist. The expectation of the creative epoch is the expectation of an artistic epoch, in which art will have the leading place in life. The artist is always a creator. Art is always a victory over the heaviness of "the world"—never adaptation to "the world." The act of art is directly opposed to every sort of added burden—in art there is liberation. The essential in artistic creativity is victory over the burden of necessity. . . . In the creative-artistic attitude towards this world we catch a glimpse of another world. To receive this world unto oneself in beauty is to break through the deformity of "this world" into another. The world which is forced upon us, "this world" is deformed, it is not cosmic, beauty is not in it. Accepting the beauty in the world unto oneself is always creativity. In freedom, not in compulsion, we attain to the beauty of the world. In every artistic activity a new world is created, the cosmos, a world enlightened and free. The scruf falls from the face of the world. Artistic creativity is ontological rather than psychological in its nature.[22]

Robinson understood himself and his poetry to be an emanation of this creative urge. But while modern poetry, drawing its impetus from this conviction that the world is an aesthetic phenomenon, has been consistently iconoclastic, his has never seemed so. It appears at first glance quite timid, cautious, and safe. This appearance is deceiving, however. The creative urge is as much present in his work as that of any other modern poet, but because intellect retained a respectable status in it—indeed, acts as a moderator (in both senses of the word) for spirit—it appears conventional. The real difference between Robinson's iconoclastic poetry and more demonstratively iconoclastic poetry is that his is devoted to creation, not destruction. It lacks malice and hate, the brutal will to negate or annihilate as an end in itself. From the earliest moment in his career, he aspired, instead, to construct, and at his worst was never more than decreative.[23] His unitive urge led him to poetry, where he sensed the conjunctive powers of the imagination to import holistic order to whatever it touched. Once there, understanding it more profoundly and remaining truer to or more consistent with its "laws" than most modern poets, and surpassed in these matters by none, he put its conjunctive powers to work rationalizing mysticism,[24] binding intellect and imagination together in a living realization. He wrote a poetry, consequently, which confirms and is confirmed by reality—a truly creative poetry deriving its power from and participating in a creative universe. The nature and significance of poetry, he learned by living it through to its final truth, is the inevitable truth of such a creative world. So neither whim nor opinion, not even, ultimately, taste or morality, corrupts the bond uniting his poetry with reality. Their correspondence is complete: the necessity of one is the necessity of the other. And from this bond it derives an undiminishable cogency and stature.

Naturalistic poetry

The poem of the mind in the act of
   finding
What will suffice. It has not always
   had
To find: the scene was set; it repeated
   what
Was in the script.
            Then the Theatre was changed
To something else. Its past was a souvenir.

Wallace Stevens

There is adventure here [in America],
and a welcome for novelty.

Alfred North Whitehead

In "New England," which appears in the relatively late
volume *Dionysus in Doubt* (1925), Robinson characterized
the province of American life in which he was born and reared
and in which he wrote his poetry:

> Here where the wind is always north-north-east
> And children learn to walk on frozen toes,
> Wonder begets an envy of all those

134

Who boil elsewhere with such a lyric yeast
Of love that you will hear them at a feast
Where demons would appeal for some repose,
Still clamoring where the chalice overflows
And crying wildest who have drunk the least.
Passion is here a soilure of the wits,
We're told, and Love a cross for them to bear;
Joy shivers in the corner where she knits
And Conscience always has the rocking-chair,
Cheerful as when she tortured into fits
The first cat that was ever killed by Care.   [900]

Perhaps unwittingly, but nevertheless inevitably and with equal accuracy, the poem also characterizes Robinson's poetry: like New England, whose voice it is, his poetry is deficient in passion, love, or joy, these having been killed, or all but killed, by conscience and care.

This fact is so readily apparent that almost every critic who has written on Robinson has commented on it. Louis Untermeyer, for one, said,

It is not that he is devious in the way he gives himself, but that, in the sense of a complete abandon to an emotion, he never gives himself at all. The reader feels the lack of surrender, and it is this insufficiency which keeps Robinson from joining the small company of those whose lines not only smiled their ironies in cryptic meditation or sang their loveliness beneath their breath, but also leaped and raged and bled and suffered with their creator.[1]

Making the same point with different language, Edward Sapir remarked,

Robinson's comment on life is too icy for bulk. His interest in the color and detail of the human scene is too languid to save his work from a cumulative monotony. His art does not, in any deeply valid sense, reflect life . . . it sets in nearly always where life has unravelled itself and is waiting for its tart, ironic epitaph.[2]

Though also sensitive to the presence of conscience and care, Charles Cestre, contrary to Untermeyer and Sapir, applauded their effect on Robinson's poetry and identified its presiding censor when he said that Robinson

stands at variance with what has been called the "insurgent" movement in contemporary American literature. If we readers of the
twentieth century lent ourselves unreservedly to the influence of a
number of writings that claim to mirror the modern spirit, we might
cease to believe that the greatness of man is to be a rational being. A
large part of the literature of today seems to have become a free field
for impulse to romp in, with sensation and sensuality as companions.
Reason and conscience undergo an eclipse . . . we might think we
are living in a pandemonium of mad appetite and crazy fantasy.[3]

Robinson's poetry, written from the same bias as Cestre's remark, is indeed committed to the idea of man as a moral and
rational being. For this reason Robinson did not, like Whitman,
delight in the flesh, the mass of men, nature, the things of this
world. Nor did he find anything of value in impulse, the gustier
passions, sexual love, the procreative urge.

To be sure, passion, love, and joy are not totally absent
from Robinson's poetry. *Tristram,* for instance, is a retelling of
the classic love story, and Fernando Nash, of *The Man Who
Died Twice,* has a religious experience:

> . . . and a vast joy,
> Which broke and swept and covered him like a sea
> Of innocence, leaving him eager as a child
> That has outlived experience and remembers
> Only the golden moment as it flows,
> Told him in silence that was more than speech
> That after passion, arrogance and ambition,
> Doubt, fear, defeat, sorrow and desperation,
> He had wrought out of martyrdom the peace
> That passeth understanding. [943]

But this is a transcendent joy, an ecstasy issuing from the
reduction of life to its austere spiritual essence, not a joy of life
such as that referred to in "New England." More importantly,
though Nash breaks free of all the bonds prohibiting mystical release, the poem does not; for Nash's experience, related second-
hand by a narrator—who, indeed, speaks of himself as "making several entrances with his determinism" (956)—is observed
from a spectator's point of view. Consequently, the emphasis in
the poem falls less on Nash's experience than it does on the

rator's relation to Nash. By means of mutual compassion
[ ] trust the narrator comes to know and value Nash's human-
[ ] and thereby discovers the deeper reaches of his own spiritual
[ ]; but the poem, as its form and especially its ending make
[ ]ar, is a reflection on the mystical experience, a dialogue of
[ ]e man's consciousness with another man's vital being. Unable
[ ] know this vital being firsthand, the narrator refuses to commit himself categorically to Nash's interpretation of his experience. Though he proclaims, "I believe / Today that all he told
me for the truth / Was true" (957), he nevertheless prefaces his
confession with the remark, "To each his own credulity, I
say, / And ask as much" (956). He sympathizes with and he
believes, but he cannot be certain—his reason is unable to
comprehend or prove Nash's claims. And so it is with the poem.
The cautious tone of the concluding passage as well as the point
of view and emphasis in the poem—the fact that Nash's mystical experience is not allowed to stand triumphantly alone—
leaves no doubt that the joy is remotely perceived. Like *Tristram*, wherein love is not passionately proclaimed but cau-
tiously assessed, this poem does not so much joyously affirm a
profound spiritual experience as view it from the cool perspective of the mind. Thus, though joy and love and passion, both
worldly and spiritual, occur in Robinson's poetry, they never
dominate it. Never does Robinson's poetry sing; never does it
become a vehicle for the direct expression of agony or ecstasy; it
is always missing "the final note of passion." [4]

The absence of the lyrical from Robinson's poetry, too
obvious to be missed by even the casual reader, was not an
oversight; he deliberately, or rather from necessity, excluded it.
Though an avid devotee of the theatre, Robinson nevertheless
disliked comic opera, of which he said, "I do not care for that
kind of celebration—for it always seems to be a celebration of
some kind." [5] He explained why that kind of celebration never
occurs in his poetry when he wrote, to William Vaughn Moody,
whom he critized for getting too much color in his poetry, "I am
what I am, and therefore I have my own paint pots to dabble
with. Blacks and grays and browns and blues for the most

137

part—but also a trick, I hope, of letting the white come through
in places." [6] The trick of letting the white come through depended, in fact, on his deliberately using somber paint. As
Robinson had the speaker of "Credo" say, he

> welcomes when he fears,
> The black and awful chaos of the night;
> For through it all—above, beyond it all—
> I know the far-sent message of the years,
> I feel the coming glory of the Light.   [94]

Passion, love, color, sensory delights, the joy of life—these
compete with the white by drawing attention to the things of
this world and the flesh, their brightness obscuring or flooding
out the light of the transcendent spiritual reality behind them.
Robinson welcomed the black and awful chaos of the night
because only when the luster of the materialistic world and the
flesh are obscured can the far-sent message come through. In
effect, he chose renunciation in the sense and for the same
reasons Emily Dickinson did when she wrote,

> Renunciation—is a piercing Virtue—
> The letting go
> A presence—for an Expectation—
> Not now—
> The putting out of Eyes—
> Just Sunrise—
> Lest Day—
> Day's Great Progenitor—
> Outvie
> Renunciation—is the Choosing
> Against itself—
> Itself to justify
> Unto itself—
> When larger function—
> Make that appear—
> Smaller—that Covered Vision—Here— [7]

The far-sent message, identified with the Light, not with the
iridescent hues of life, is perceptible only if sensory delight and
worldly passion are renounced, only if the glittering mask of
phenomena is blacked out. The soul can emerge only when the
essential in man eclipses the accidental.

Had Robinson been able to attain completely th[?]
aspiration—a spiritual realization of things and th[?]
cance through the coming of the Light in its full glo[?]
poetry, totally free of contamination by the colors of the wo[?]
would have radiated an icy, pure whiteness. Or he might even
have soared into that mystical center Santayana envisaged when
he said,

There would not be a universe worshipped, but a universe praying;
and the flame of the whole fire, the whole seminal and generative
movement of nature, would be the love of God. This love would be
erotic; it would be really love, and not something wingless called by
that name. It would bring celestial glimpses not to be retained but
culminating in moments of unspeakable rapture, in a union with all
good, in which the soul would vanish as an object because, as an
organ, it had found its perfect employment.[8]

But he was not disposed to identify the Light with the erotic or
to drive through to this ultimate consummation, a transcendence of the here and now into absolute, ecstatic spiritual freedom and perfection. As a realist, a man viewing things as they
are within the world he inhabits, he experienced the transcendent extreme as one element among several in the human
economy and gave it its place and no more.

Sometimes he gave the impression that he sought ultimate
consummation. In what, for instance, is probably the angriest
moment of his life, at least in his published writing, he violently
attacked the curtailment of freedom effected by Prohibition. It
was at this time that he wrote most of the poems in *Dionysus in
Doubt*, including "New England," and in this volume is to be
found his most explicit, if not his only, didactic poetry of the
last half of his career, a poetry which directly attacks social-
political conditions in contemporary America. His mood at this
time is expressed most trenchantly in his letters, where he wrote
on one occasion of "Dionysus in Doubt," "It had to come out,
for it [the poem] had been accumulating in me ever since the
hypocritical (or worse) action of the so-called Supreme Court
on the constitutionality of a certain much to be damned amendment"; [9] and on another,

I don't see the independence of an alleged democracy that will accept the eighteenth amendment without general secession or civil war. The worst feature of it all is that the people don't seem to see that such a thing is fundamentally evil and arbitrary, and therefore cannot work for good.[10]

Robinson was not simply protecting his own access to alcohol, or anyone else's, for having once been a heavy drinker, he knew the curse of alcoholism well. Rather, he was arguing for freedom and all that it makes possible. Dionysus says:

> "Sometimes I wonder what machine
> Your innocence will employ,
>
> .   .   .   .
> When all are niched and ticketed and all
> Are standardized and unexceptional,
> To perpetuate complacency and joy
> Of uniform size and strength
> Sometimes I ponder whether you have seen,
> Or contemplated over much down there,
> The treacherous ways that you are now pursuing,
> Or by just what immeasurable expense
> Of unexplained omnipotence
> You are to make it lead you anywhere
> Than to the wonder of a sick despair
> That waits upon a gullible undoing."   [866]

What mattered to Robinson was the opportunity for each man to realize "the truth toward which he was tending" (152). In *Roman Bartholow,* published two years before *Dionysus in Doubt,* he had announced the existence of freedom as a metaphysical fact, and throughout the last half of his career he reiterated the conviction that every man, caught in the egocentric predicament, must discover the Light on his own, in his own way. But the truth toward which he himself was tending was identified with poetry, so that his defense of freedom was a defense of poetry, of himself and his career, and of the life of the spirit in a materialistic universe and society. To defend these, which are not commonplace matters, he had to argue for the nonstandardized and exceptional. Dionysus, the god of wine, who is also the god of inspiration, of the spirit reaching for release and joy, represents the extreme aspiration and achievement; as a god he is ideally all that common, earthbound man is not—free, exuberant, exultant. So, in attacking an adamantly repressive society, "Dionysus in Doubt," along with "New England" and other poems in the volume, is intended to preserve man's Dionysian possibilities and to defend thereby the right of Robinson's life and art to fulfill themselves in accordance with their own necessity.

However, what he means by human freedom is not mystical release from the world but liberty within it, not escape from conscience and care but a life congruent with them. W. B. Yeats once cried out in protest against the characters in late nineteenth-century drama, "Why did they not speak out with louder voices or move with freer gestures? What was it that weighted upon their souls perpetually? Certainly they were all in a prison, and yet there was no prison." [11] Like so many of his contemporaries, Robinson inhabited such a prison; something weighed down his soul. He could not free impulse, appetite, or fantasy, nor passion, love, or joy from conscience and care. He did not even totally free the intellect. "Valéry," Elizabeth Sewell has said, "speaks of that 'Intellectual Comedy which has not yet found its poet, and which in my view would be even more precious than the Comedie Humaine, than the Divine Comedy itself.' " [12] Robinson, writing out of the intellectualism Valéry speaks for and writing eventually a "hard-nosed" intellectual comedy, did not, as a painter might say, release the mind from the object to create pure abstraction. "That which darkens man's intellect" [13] or spirit clung too tenaciously to Robinson's consciousness for the poetic impulse to be released to soar free of the world.

We have seen, for example, how he made poems out of the conflict between self and society in which the claims of society predominate; and that in his criticism of W. B. Yeats he was acutely conscious that a certain kind of poetry was to be expected in the nineteenth century, a poetry that did not make a holy show of the poet's self. Other signs of his being in a prison appear elsewhere. In *Porcupine,* written about the same time as

Van Zorn, the despondent protagonist says to a rather high-spirited nonconformist, "Men who would set the individual apart from the community are almost always disappointed." [14] This respect for external circumstances he explicitly acknowledged when he wrote, "I do not care to break any moral laws myself, and see no necessity in it." [15] He expanded on this respect for the claims of social morality when he said, after reading Thoreau's *Walking,*

> I did not quite relish what seemed to me to be a sort of glorified Thoreau cowardice all through the thing. For God's sake, says the sage, let me get away into the wilderness where I shall not have a single responsibility or the first symptom of social discipline, let me be a pickerel or a skunk cabbage, anything that will not have to meet the realities of civilization. There is a wholesomeness about some people that is positively unhealthy, and I find it in this essay. Still I am ready for Walden. [16]

Because he could not—or did not choose to—set the individual apart from the community, he accepted a morality which did not issue solely from the will to be free but also incorporated and honored the "other." And as a poet who acknowledges his responsibility to the social order, especially a materialistic one in which poetry is little valued, he felt that art and morality, the poetic impulse and conscience, had to be accommodated to one another. Clearly, although he held himself aloof from normal society and popular tasks, maintaining not a splendid but a solemn isolation and autonomy as a poet "hero," the world was very much with him and never completely released his spirit and imagination from its hold.

As a result, no open road, no infinite vistas, no spacious America exists in the world as he imagines it; the frontier has closed. His scene is always a tightly contained space—a closed room, an oppressive community, an inescapable self, a universe forever doomed to be what it now is, spirit imprisoned in life. At least this is the given condition from and against which man acts in his quest for freedom, and he can never be totally or permanently free of it, for it provides him with the necessary ground to stand on, take off from, and return to. Thus the truth toward which Robinson was tending entailed social and historical awareness, objectivity and realism (which imply a regard for the intractable otherness of the world), acceptance of limitations and acknowledgment of responsibility. Freedom is not escape from one's being as a moral creature but release and realization of it; to be free is not to transcend being a man but fully to be a man, a truly rational and moral creature. The prison he was in was that of his own being, simultaneously and inseparably aesthetic and moral. Poetry, the poet himself, life in general are not consummated in absolute freedom but are only really themselves and free when the opposites of which they are composed resist and define one another. Like Hawthorne, with whom he shared a preference for dark and gloomy atmosphere, Robinson understood the ironic relation between pride and self-sacrifice necessary to preserve the magnetic chain of humanity. Like Wallace Stevens, his younger contemporary, he instinctively knew that "to every faithful poet the faithful poem is an act of conscience." [17] But above all he had learned, perhaps from Puritanism or just the New England soil, that, as Emerson said, man's essential being is "the Moral Nature, the Law of laws whose revelations introduced greatness—yea, God himself—into the open soul." [18]

The criticism that Robinson's poetry excludes too much of life stops short, therefore, of the more profound effect conscience and care had on his poetry. Early in his career he announced the coming of the Light on the evidence of a dim feeling, and at the end of his career, though he was more certain about what he didn't know, that feeling was still dim and the Light had gotten no brighter. Not just the senses and passion but his imagination and soul as well were not freed to be exclusively or uninhibitedly themselves. In a passage where he is defining and assessing Robinson's achievement, Hermann Hagedorn writes of "Nicodemus," "Out of the unconscious, with the controls relaxed by fatigue, came this song of the intellectual mystic, who wanted to give himself wholly yet could not quite manage it." [19] I do not know Hagedorn's sources for his information regarding Robinson's state of mind while writing "Nico-

143

demus," so I do not know whether he is justified on biographical grounds in viewing the poem as an unrestrained lyrical release of Robinson's soul. Nevertheless, in the phrase "intellectual mystic" Hagedorn vividly captures the dramatic tensions not only of "Nicodemus" but of Robinson's poetry as a whole. An oxymoron, "intellectual" implying separateness and abstraction and "mystic" implying union and concrete feeling, the phrase succinctly identifies the dynamic antitheses within Robinson's life and art. Hagedorn is wrong, however, in saying that Robinson wanted to give himself wholly, yet could not quite manage it; he did give himself wholly, but the inherent contradictoriness of what he gave himself wholly to precluded a mystical transcendence of the type Hagedorn apparently had in mind. Because he associated the imagination with what Edgar Allan Poe called Truth and the Moral Sense rather than with Supernal Loveliness, he could not dissociate his soul from the mind or conscience and so it could not vanish as an object to itself; it could not soar free of consciousness.

When Robinson is criticized for excluding passion and bright colors from his poetry, it might be well to remember that of those poets among his contemporaries who did include them and thereby measured up to the critics' criteria of good poetry few are today remembered. Certainly Frost and Stevens, those poets who rank with Robinson as the greatest of their generation, gave little attention to romantic emotions; and though Stevens literally got plenty of bright colors in his poetry, they were not the colors of erotic passion or joy. Whereas, as Carlin Kindilieu has shown, the largest portion of the poetry written during the nineties was made from airy sentiments that had nothing to do with the actual currents of thought and feeling then sweeping through the minds of men,[20] Robinson did what under the circumstances could be done without pretense or falsification. "What a modern poet desires, above everything else," Wallace Stevens noted, "is to be nothing more than a poet of the present time." [21] Certainly this was true for Robinson. He once said, and it is a criticism applicable to most of his contemporaries who

144

were poets, "So far as I can make out, most people are so afraid of life that when they see it coming their first impulse is to hide behind a tree and shut their eyes." [22] He kept his eyes open, and without taking refuge in irrelevant emotion or ideas he made the ineluctable realities yield poetry, or an emotion commensurate with them. [23]

Such an achievement is no small task under any circumstances, but Robinson, living in a transitional period, suffered from the added disadvantage of straddling two worlds. He was well aware of this. He said of Thomas Sergeant Perry, and it was equally true of himself,

He knew, like many others, that the Great War had carried away with it the world that he had known, and in which he had best belonged; he knew also that time was at his heels, and that the new world would somehow take care of itself without him. He was undoubtedly more at home with his Victorian memories than with his twentieth century questionings and apprehensions. [24]

Now there can be no doubt that much of the emotion in Robinson's poetry, resulting from the dominion of conscience and care over passion, love, and joy, of reason over impulse, reflects the nineteenth century. But it is wrong to conclude from this, as some have done, that his allegiance is entirely to the nineteenth century. His claim, quoted earlier, that his spiritual and intellectual activity were all for the future but his human life all for the past is testimony that, Janus-like, he looked to the past but at the same time faced the future, forthrightly confronting his twentieth-century questionings and apprehensions. He did not despair of the new order; on occasion he spoke of America as the hope of mankind and he even thought of himself as making a contribution to the future. Appropriately for a man whose imagination was grounded in realism and committed to truth, he did not passively lament the ravages of time but changed as his understanding of reality changed, meeting the new on its own terms, accepting its creative challenge. The predominant feeling of his poetry derives from his passion to see life with absolute clarity for what it is and to conform his art intellectually and morally to its reality. As a consequence he wrote what Stevens

145

called a contemporaneous poetry, a poetry that in a deeply valid sense reflects life as he and his *avant-garde* contemporaries understood it, and therefore it is, in the end, pre-eminently modern.

Out of Robinson's compulsion to write a contemporaneous poetry eventually came a poetry of the act. As his work evolved he ran the gamut of truth, beginning with empiricism, the truth of the senses, progressing to cynicism, the intellect's active questioning of appearances, and culminating in a phenomenological acceptance of the spirit's reality. The poetry of this last stage, which bears witness to the soul's truth and power, consummates, I repeat, Robinson's lifetime effort to be rid of materialistic dualism, the form that the dominant modern Western intellectual tradition—fathered by Descartes and perpetuated by continental rationalism, British empiricism, sensation psychology, and positivistic science—took in the last decades of the nineteenth century in America.

Descartes's skepticism had driven a wedge between spiritual and material substance, dissociating intellect from nature and giving the former priority over the latter. The consequent tyranny over life by the mind, and it amounted to no less than that, produced, over the course of several centuries, the commonly observed disproportionate progress between scientific and technological achievements and moral development. It also produced what is probably history's greatest irony—man, who had come to feel himself a stranger in this world, outdid nature, creating with his intelligence and supposedly in his own image an even more strange and estranging environment. Given hegemony, the mind legislated a universe and created a social world compatible with itself—abstract, logical, and mechanical—but uncongenial to emotion, passion, and spirit. With man's interior life so alienated from the external world, the mind so abstracted from organic processes, the head and the heart became bitter foes, with the head, the favored and the aggressor, refusing to sanction the heart's aspiration or provide it with a confirming environment. Impotent and passive, deeply imprisoned in a cold world, an inert body, and dull senses, the spirit, as Edgar Allan Poe poignantly recorded in his poetry and theory, was forced to regard itself either contemptuously, as without nobility or meaning, or with melancholy, and then preciously nurse its sorrowful longing to return to its home in a remote heaven. Unable to get moral support from the mind and so be valued, there was nothing in this world for the spirit to live by or for; and with nothing to hope for but release and Christianity receding, so no place to be released to, it was impotent. Descartes's dualism, stopping up the springs of spiritual life with matter and mechanism, destroyed the spirit's freedom, and the mind, unwilling to believe in the spirit, even went so far as to demand its death.

Robinson was not a David doing combat with the Goliath of materialism; he was not shaping a new and living pattern all alone. The war in defense of spirit so that it might live again had been going on, in fact, for at least a century by the time he began writing, the Romantics in Europe, England, and America having begun it by attacking rationalism, empiricism, neoclassicism, and science. And the frontal attack by the Romantics had been supported by a flanking movement in science itself, where biology, gaining the ascendant over physics as a force in Western intellectual life, turned attention from the mechanical to the vital. By the last decades of the century biology had advanced so far as to capture the minds of such major philosophers as Bergson and William James, who took their assumptions from it rather than from physics. Then, toward the end of the century, under the impact of developments in mathematics and the study of physical phenomena, physics itself began to look toward biology for its assumptions, and a philosopher such as Alfred North Whitehead, a mathematician and physicist by training, could take his models for the physical world from the life sciences. The progress of the war altered the balance of power and made possible in Robinson's lifetime a new skepticism, more radical than Descartes's, aimed at undermining the authority he gave to mind and elevating feeling to an equal or superior position. In America the war against Descartes's dualism and the new skepticism, prepared for by Jonathan Edwards' defense of a divine and supernatural light, which was intended to justify the powers of spirit against the claims of sensational psychology, began in earnest with Emerson's call for establishing the original relation with the universe and returning to the essential man.

The intellectual landmark, and companion to Robinson's poetry, in the attack on Descartes's dualism within modern thought, as a whole as well as in the nineties, is Santayana's *Skepticism and Animal Faith*. Here Western thought, especially since Descartes, is systematically shown to be based on half-hearted doubt. Elsewhere Santayana had subjected himself to Descartes's exercise in doubt and discovered ultimate reality to be power or, as Wallace Stevens, avid reader of Santayana, stated it in more personal form, "Modern reality is the reality of decreation in which our revelations are not the revelations of belief, but the precious portent of our own powers. The greatest truth we can hope to discover . . . is that man's truth is the final resolution of everything." [25] What Stevens means by man's truth is explained by Unamuno, like Santayana a Spanish philosopher-poet, who also put himself through an exercise in doubt and discovered the same reality Santayana did:

I have sought to strip naked, not only my own soul, but the human soul, be its nature what it may, its destiny to disappear or not to disappear. And we have arrived at the bottom of the abyss, at the irreconcilable conflict between reason and vital feeling. And having arrived here, I have told you that it is necessary to accept the conflict as such and to live by it.[26]

Unamuno even said at one point, "I do not wish to make peace between my heart and my head, between my faith and my reason—I wish rather that there should be a war between them." [27] For the spirit to live, a new world, based on a different foundation than Descartes's, had to be built. That is what Robinson, along with Santayana, Stevens, and Unamuno, was driving toward—not simply a correction of deficiencies within the established structure, but a complete replacement of it.

At the center of experience for Robinson, then, was a war,

powers in active conflict with each other, and in perpetuating that war he and Unamuno were only affirming the ineluctable reality to which their doubt led them. Now warfare is possible only if both antagonists possess a certain strength, and it can be sustained only if they are equipped with resources sufficient to keep one from unconditionally defeating the other, a quite different relation between reason and vital feeling than that laid down by Descartes. For Unamuno, for the new skepticism in general, and for Robinson the unquestionably real was the sensation of being arising from the dynamic interaction which takes place between reason and vital feeling. Organic process, not reducible to any simpler element within or without itself, is the given, the starting point of experience and knowledge. If man's truth, as Stevens said, is the final resolution of everything, then reality is a vital tension between opposites. What is left when the accidental has been stripped away is change, process, striving, activity, creativity.

Descartes's principle, "I think, therefore I am," is replaced in the new thought, in the reconstruction of philosophy, and in Robinson's poetry by "I act (which implies desires, resistance, and assertion), therefore I am." Since vital feeling is given metaphysical priority by the new thought, the key to truth in the new world lies in the nature of life, which is the primordial fact and supreme value. Santayana defined what "life" meant to Robinson and the nineties as well as to himself when he said:

We should explain motion and life rather by their purpose and end, by that unrealized ideal which moving and living things seem to aspire to, and may be said to love. What justifies itself is not any fact or law; for why should these not have been different? What justifies itself is what is good, what is as it ought to be. But things in motion, Aristotle conceived, declare, as it were, that they are not satisfied, and ought to be in some different condition. They look to a fulfillment which is as yet ideal. This fulfillment, if it included motion and life, could include them inwardly only; it would consist in a sustained activity, never lapsing or suffering change. Such an activity is the unchanging goal towards which life advances and by which its different states are measured.[28]

Life in general is purposive activity—the oak, sparrow, or horse seeks to fulfill its distinctive destiny. Activated by self-generated needs and by inherent powers, life seeks fruition of a potential latent within itself. Human life is endowed with the additional faculty of consciousness, which permits teleological awareness. Through imagination and his power to act, man can spin visions out of himself, project them ahead as ideas and ideals, then be magnetically drawn toward a realization of them. George Bernard Shaw, proponent of the Life Force, linking human life with life in general in an evolutionary chain, has Don Juan in *Man and Superman* excitedly proclaim,

Are we agreed that Life is a force which has made innumerable experiments in organizing itself; that the mammoth and the moth, the mouse and the megatherium, the flies and the Fathers of the Church, are all more or less successful attempts to build up that raw force into higher and higher individuals, the ideal individual being omnipotent, omniscient, infallible, and withal completely, unilludedly self-conscious: in short, a god? [29]

Don Juan's question, however, is not much more than a vigorous dramatic utterance of what the pragmatists said more commonly about perception and thought and Robinson sought to achieve in and through his poetry. Perception, thought, and art are activities within the overall action of a live creature to secure the satisfactions it by nature seeks from the world in which it finds itself. The new skepticism, free of "contempt for the body, fear of the senses, and the opposition of flesh to spirit," [30] acknowledged the life process as ultimate fact and value, and thereby freed spirit from the death's-row cell in which it had been placed by materialism and mechanism to be a living force in the world.

Now the poetry of the act does not begin with Robinson. Its inception lies in Emerson's call for a poet and poetry capable of articulating a reality characterized by power, process, freedom, and creative thrust. Emerson brought indigenous American voluntarism, subterranean before his time, to the surface in his work, and urged others to join him in creating a thought and art consistent with it. To satisfy Emerson's demand, poetry

150

would have to be based on the assumption that "the soul active sees absolute truth and utters truth, or creates," [31] for in a world of power ultimate reality lies not in outward form or abstract concept but in the mysterious, intangible forces governing change, growth, and metamorphosis. Since reality is located within, the poet must turn himself inside out, giving objective form in poetry to his interior life—which is why so many of the great works in American literature are autobiographical. And since man's condition can be understood only if "he acts it as life, before he apprehends it as truth," [32] since, that is, the interior life, characterized by power and activity, can reveal itself only while active, an appropriate poetry would have to embody that process or at least point to and applaud it. Whichever it did, by its very nature poetry would participate in a "strange process . . . by which experience is converted into thought. . . . The new deed is yet part of life,—remains for a time immersed in our unconscious life. In some contemplative hour it detaches itself from the life like a ripe fruit, to become a thought in the mind. Instantly it is raised, transfigured . . . ." [33] What Emerson called for, then, was a poetry of self-knowledge leading to awareness of the potent spiritual reality within the individual, an articulation of the absolute truth within man which would release the spirit to be more freely and successfully active. This call has been answered in literature not only by the poetry of Whitman, Robinson, Stevens, Frost, Cummings, and Williams, to mention only the established names, but by Thoreau, Melville, and Henry Miller in prose. And the efforts of these literary voices to give body to America's indigenous voluntarism have been supplemented in philosophy by pragmatism, "the distinctively American philosophy." [34]

Whitman is usually cited as the first to answer Emerson's call for a distinctively American poet, one who could capture in poetic form the qualities of a dynamic reality. Certainly he solved in poetry, as Thoreau did in narrative prose, the problems of literary form for organic art in America. And his poetry more obviously than Emerson's does what it professes. At its best, in poems such as "Crossing Brooklyn Ferry," "Out of the

Cradle Endlessly Rocking," or "Passage to India," it not only makes statements about sympathy, identity, or spiritual adventuring, but it performs acts of reaching out and touching, of plummeting to its own center, or of striking out on a spiritual voyage. These poems are what they do, not what they say. But Whitman only writes a different poetry of the act, not the first.

If Emerson's tendency to exalt thought and identify it with will and spirit is kept in mind, his own poetry will be seen as performing that strange process by which the unconscious is elevated into thought. Certainly it points to and applauds the potent spiritual reality within man and behind a poem. The difference between Whitman and Emerson is that, while both take activity as absolute, one locates the active power in the procreative urge or love and writes poems based structurally upon the dynamics of passion, while the other locates it in the disembodied intellect or soul and writes poems in "logical" forms reflecting the mind's preference for conceptualized order. They view the organic process from opposite poles, thus giving somewhat different emphases to the tension between power and form, and in doing so initiate antithetical traditions within the poetry of the act.

But like most romantics, and unlike Robinson, Frost, and Stevens, both suffer from a repudiation of analytic thought and learning, necessary because of the strategic disadvantage in their quarrel with Newtonian science and Lockeian psychology, those doctrines which held the reflective intellect captive in their time. To win freedom for the spirit, which had been thoroughly denigrated in Descartes's dualism, they had to demand unconditional defeat of its enemy. Consequently, the romantics in America as well as in England and on the continent relied heavily upon intuition and sentiment, which when dissociated from intellect were unstable and prone to emotional mysticism and sentimentality. They were also easy prey to Victorianism, classicism, and realism, reactions against dissolving intellect in feeling and passion, because they had the mind's allegiance to materialism on their side and could keep the spirit and imagination on the intellectual defensive.

The warfare between reason and vital feeling in Robinson's poetry does not perpetuate Descartes's dualism and so is not vulnerable to the weaknesses inherent in its heavy favoritism toward the mind; it does not force either-or antitheses between reason and vital feeling and so discourages taking one extreme or another or fluctuating insanely between them. The Descartian absolute dichotomy in which vital feeling is excluded from this world is replaced by a compromise in which reason, though the loser, does not unconditionally surrender to feeling. The world of vital feeling extends a tolerance to reason that materialism denied it, rejecting the false dichotomy which absolutely severs them and granting a working interdependence between the irreconcilable antagonists. This neoromanticism, if I dare risk that term, respects the intellect and in turn is intellectually respectable. The mind's loyalty is transferred to life, reason becoming subordinated to life's purposes and serving as an instrument in the search by the Life-Force, as Shaw referred to it, for organization through consciousness and higher individuals. As exemplified by the protagonists in Robinson's late long poems, reason participates in the living process without losing or betraying its identity. In fact, the vital and spiritual are so interfused that the mind sometimes is looked upon as a living organ inseparable in man from his vital being.

Obviously this conception of a working relation between mind and spirit is pragmatic; all the powers of the mind function as instruments for more effective activity. Emerson, assuming the subject-object dichotomy of a pronounced idealist with a rage for monism, sharply diminished the role played by the real—by what Stevens called the pressure of reality—in the vital activity he wanted to represent accurately and promulgate the truth about. Still influenced by Descartes's dualistic ways, he had categorically to oppose understanding, or analytical and conceptualizing thought, to organic thought (intuition or reason). These poles repel each other and so produce no current. Since they are disjunctively related, Emerson found it difficult to explain activity in his voluntaristic world, because when all the power lies with spirit, flowing from some vague inexhaustible source through the soul or thought, and none lies with matter, then the generative source is hidden in mysticism. In Robinson's voluntarism, the real as well as the ideal has a positive function in activity. The will is not a steady stream flowing from a vague inexhaustible source; instead, it is a current or energy generated by poles carrying opposite charges and in proximity to one another. For Robinson, power flows through all the faculties, each in aspiring toward its perfection reflecting the upward drive of the organism as a whole and life in general. In Robinson's view the real plays its necessary role opposite the ideal, which in turn plays its necessary role against the real. Intellect enters into the life of the imagination and poetry, and they in turn enter into its life. Whereas the mind translates the soul's purposes into worldly possibilities according to circumstances and available alternatives, the soul keeps the mind from becoming rigid, each assisting in the sustenance of the other and staying alive through mutual support. To be man, to be and act, Robinson's poetry finally proclaims, is to be constituted of such opposites and to be energized by the power generated at their crossway. That is the human condition in this world, and that is the truth proclaimed by the poetry of the act as Robinson practiced it.

Again Santayana provides the best explanation of this new relation between reason and vital feeling and of the character and aims of the poetry of the act as Robinson practiced it. In his discussion of Lucretius in *Three Philosophical Poets,* he writes,

The poetry we see in nature is due to the emotion the spectacle produces in us, the life of nature might be as romantic and sublime as it chose, it would be dust and ashes to us if there were nothing sublime and romantic in ourselves to be stirred by it to sympathy. But our emotion may be ingenuous; it may be concerned with what nature really is and does, has been and will do forever. It need not arise from a selfish preoccupation with what these immense realities involve for our own persons or may be used to suggest to our self-indulgent fancy. No, the poetry of nature may be discerned merely by the power of intuition which it awakens and the understanding which it employs. These faculties, more, I should say, than our moodiness or stuffy dreams, draw taut the strings of the soul,

154

and bring out her full vitality and music. Naturalism is a philosophy of observation, and of an imagination that extends the observable; all the sights and sounds of nature enter into it, and lend it their directness, pungency, and coercive stress. At the same time, naturalism is an intellectual philosophy; it divines substance behind appearance, continuity behind change, law behind fortune. It therefore attaches all those sights and sounds to a hidden background that connects and explains them. So understood, nature has depth as well as sensuous variety. Before the sublimity of this insight, all forms of the pathetic fallacy seem cheap and artificial. Mythology, that to a childish mind is the only possible poetry, sounds like bad rhetoric in comparison. The naturalistic poet abandons fairyland, because he has discovered nature, history, the actual passions of man. His imagination has reached maturity; its pleasure is to dominate, not to play.[35]

Not all of what Santayana says here applies to Robinson's poetry—for instance, all the sights and sounds of nature do not enter into it. But though he favors the intellectual over the empirical side of naturalism in some respects, Robinson does write a naturalistic poetry as it is defined here by Santayana.[36] He abandons fairyland for the actualities of life and seeks to understand man in depth, to divine the higher law underlying the variety and accidents of his existence.[37]

Robinson differs from Lucretius in that Lucretius subjected man along with the rest of nature to the principles governing the Democritean universe, the chance and mechanical association of atoms; while Robinson, in accordance with the dualism between material nature and organic life he inherited from materialism, regarded the vital or spiritual as a separate mode of existence. Where Lucretius gave sole credence to what William James called the disjunctive aspects of experience, Robinson emphasized the conjunctive ones. But employing the empirical, intellectual approach of naturalism, and seeking a reduction of life to the necessary and sufficient conditions of its existence or the most "abstract" truth about man's being, Robinson sought a rational comprehension of the vital for what it is in and of itself. Like Lucretius, he wanted to free men, including himself, of illusion and superstition through a candid knowl-

155

edge of life so that they could live without fear and trembling. Amaranth, the symbolic voice of truth, announces this aim to Fargo:

> To a few
> I murmur not in vain: they fly from here
> As you did, and I see no more of them
> Where, far from this miasma of delusion
> They know the best there is for man to know;
> They know the peace of reason.   [1392]

The peace of reason, Robinson's parallel to Santayana's idea of maturity, comes from rational insight entailing simultaneously a recognition of things as they are and acceptance of man's place in the world.

Santayana clarifies the character and aims of the poetry of the act as Robinson practiced it in the *Life of Reason,* where he is speaking theoretically for himself rather than describing the works of another writer. "If a poet," he writes,

could clarify the myth he begins with, so as to reach ultimate scientific notions of nature and life, he would still be animated by vivid feeling and its imaginative expression. Tragic, fatal, intractable, he might well feel that the truth was; but these qualities have never been absent from that half-mythical world through which poets, for want of a rational education, have hitherto wandered. A rational poet's vision would have the same moral function which myth was asked to fulfill, and fulfilled so treacherously. Such a poet would no doubt need a robust genius. If he possessed it, and in transmitting all existence falsified nothing, giving that picture of everything which human experience in the end would have drawn, he would achieve an ideal result. In prompting mankind to imagine, he would be helping them to live. His poetry, without ceasing to be a fiction in its method and ideality, would be an ultimate truth in its practical scope. It would present in graphic images the total efficacy of surrounding things. Such a poetry would be more deeply rooted in human nature than in any casual fancy, and therefore more appealing to the heart. The images it had worked out would confront passion more intelligibly than does the world as at present conceived, with its mechanism half ignored and its ideality half invented. . . .[38]

Naturalistic poetry as defined by Santayana or the poetry of the act as practiced by Robinson is without gods or myth; it is a rational poetry dedicated to presenting graphic images of reality, which includes ideality, man's vital interest in his own purposes, within its naturalistic framework. Such images resemble scientific models of nature and their truth frees the spirit to act; that is, by offering an accurate map for what is in the world and how to get to it they perform a moral and therefore a practical function, permitting consciousness to distinguish more accurately the proper ends of vital feeling and guide it efficiently to them. Transfiguring unconscious experience into thought or conscious awareness, naturalistic poetry facilitates the conduct of life in this world by its contribution to life's search for higher organization. Imagination, participating in experience, illuminates facts and possibility, thereby promoting life's enlargement.

Such a poetry is not a cynosure completely absorbing attention in itself, an autonomous structure of words held in suspension by irony, ambiguity, paradox, and tension. This kind of poetry and the poetry of the act are both based upon the concept of a "field," fundamental in the new thought; but where the poem is a field unto itself for the New Criticism, for the poetry of the act it is an entity and power within the field of life. It is engaged, not dissociated; it directs attention to life and operates within the world. In doing that it imitates nature, not in the classical sense of representation, but in William Carlos Williams' meaning of the phrase in his remark that when imitating nature "we then ourselves become nature, and so invent an object which is an extension of the process." [39] It imitates by doing as nature does, by being natural and thus creative, by participating in the continual flux and perhaps upward thrust of decreation and creation that permeates a universe in process. Whereas a good New Critical poem, one by T. S. Eliot for example, grounds itself in a literary tradition and requires a cultivated familiarity with and response to it, a Robinson poem insists on an encounter with reality. Although the poem is a creation, the accent in the poem nevertheless tends to be on decreation. Robinson, Frost, and Stevens, following the lead of Emerson, Thoreau, and Whitman, write about the return of the spirit or imagination to its source in life—Robinson designating it the law of life; Frost, the pasture or spring, as in "Directive"; Stevens, the rock. By dissolution and backward movement, present form is sloughed off and the mind is recharged with power to create. In touch with its source, reason transcends its finite forms and is free to act morally; integrated with its source, consciousness can serve its "ground"; put back into experience, imagination can give a new and living pattern to life.

The accent on decreation in Robinson's poetry is inevitable because the act, as distinct from inertia, has its origin in that precise explosive moment when, magically, the spirit becomes free of necessity. What Robinson's poetry of the act bears witness to is the capacity of life at this moment, the moment of inception or inspiration, for regeneration. Zest, excitement, adventure are at their peak when, suddenly, miraculously free of matter, guilt, habit, the past, the old, life can begin anew. Then confidence and belief, purpose, freedom, and vigor buoy up the spirit, which can breathe deeply, expand, and delight in its liberation. Spontaneous, elastic, graceful at this moment, life springs back, reborn after burrowing into and burying the "Me." The poetry of the act is ultimately, then, like all the literature in the Emerson tradition, an art of beginnings—of dawn, spring, and youth, of morning, novelty, and adventure; it is characterized by a metaphysical realism in which through a return to its source via an annihilation of finite forms, innocence is regained, joy abounds, and activity results.

This is not to say that every poem or poet is overtly joyous or comic. Robinson obviously is not. There are degrees of overtness. Some poets, or rather some imaginations, are younger and more virile than others; certainly Stevens' is more so than Robinson's. But whether solemn or exuberant, and no matter how pronounced the conventional forms—and they prevail in Robinson's poetry—and regardless of point of view, whether disposed toward the procreative urge or thought, vital feeling or reason, the poetry of the act calls attention to and is a sign of life's redemptive power present in man. Harboring decreative energy within a created form, embracing the two poles of mind and spirit, constituted of and issuing from the tension between them, this poetry like a phoenix rises from its own ashes and exemplifies the diastolic-systolic rhythm of life in all its phases, in the life of reason, love, and the imagination, for example, as well as in the life of the body. Though outwardly saturnine, in its heart of hearts Robinson's poetry of the act reveals through its "graphic image" of natural reality that regardless how deeply the soul may lie beneath the surface of the mind, it is there, the power and the glory, the free and freeing "truth," and its light will prevail even in the dark and awful chaos of the night.

Freedom within the world, escape from inertia, is the essence of Robinson's poetry. But all poetry, as an instrument of the human spirit, results from the aspiration to be free, from the spirit's profound need to find its voice; and it frees by equipping consciousness with an idea of the specific location, character, and possibility of freedom. Though all poetry perforce defines freedom, the definitions range widely (from absolute, otherworldly forms to finite animal and social liberties within this world) and are qualified by an infinite variety of emotional attitudes or states (such as hope and despair, joy and melancholy) in simple or complex forms, depending upon whether freedom is within reach, remote but nevertheless attainable, or impossible. In Robinson's poetry of the act, as in all poetry, the imagination, relating the self to the world by means of its "instinctive integrations," frees by creating consciousness, both for the poet and his reader, through the aesthetic use of language; but this poetry stands apart from other kinds in that it calls attention to itself as an exercise of vital powers and encourages their exercise here and now. It is intended to affect the quality of worldly life.

Since it does not directly transform a natural raw material into new physical entities, poetry is sometimes regarded as nothing more than a sideline commentator on the march of real events. Working upon words, human creations to begin with, spinning phantasies from language, itself a phantasy, the poet makes no difference in nature, neither rearranging nor adding anything to it. But even if language is an artifact rather than natural raw material, men, Robinson knew from his vocation if nothing else, live in and through it. Aware that imagination plays an active role in shaping what men want and how they go after it, he never doubted poetry's power to affect the way men perceive and interpret their world. He did not need a psychologist, armed with Gestalt theory or perception experiments, to verify that. He was by nature and vocation a creator, and he acted in accordance with his light, finding freedom and joy in its true source—not the altered environment, but the active soul. His poetry, like all poetry, shapes our attitudes and arouses our passion. It confronts us with a vision and embodiment of the good and chides us to emulate its example. But Robinson would teach his readers by the example of his protagonists that the luminous moment made possible by poetry is not an end or end in itself but a liberating and initiating stimulus.

Robinson's poetry, along with Frost's and Stevens', is very much an expression of the nineties' progressivism in its affirmation of activity. His poetry verifies that what is real and valuable, as it must be for progress to be anything more than an illusion, is the power in man to imagine and to work successfully toward a more perfect life. In this way his poetry helps to clarify and justify its industrial achievements and hopes, its faith in the new world and the new man it was making, and its enthusiasm for the emerging national identity, modern, free of the past. For an era committed to adventure and achievement, he wrote an appropriately masculine poetry, not devoid of compassion, conscience, and care, but nevertheless little invaded by feminine qualities. While shunning naive optimism, it gives us the best of the energy and aspiration running through that era's social as well as intellectual life.

When it speaks for this vitality and orientation toward the future, toward the better world that can be, Robinson's poetry, though it is not as obviously public or forensic nor as evidently disposed toward the rough-hewn, open, and expansive forms (in opposition to the well-wrought urn) as that of more exuberant American wirters, cannot help but reflect the overall sweep of American culture. Emerson first, then Thoreau, Whitman.

160

and others, unwilling to surrender the scene to historical forces or crass animal energy, vigorously insisted that poetry play its key role in the making of America. To that end, they created and encouraged a literary art, a product of the active spirit, that would put intelligence, conscience, and soul into the nation. Robinson's poetry, written within the tradition of this aspiration, more commonly present in the continuing drive in America to produce, to be making and doing, to be active and busy, embodies its impulse toward a more completely moral and spiritual world. It exalts that freedom which Americans herald as the definitive element in their personality and culture.

Moreover, in furthering and celebrating freedom Robinson was extending the religious adventure brought to this land by the Puritans. The European in general, excitedly setting out from the old country with his highly cultivated intelligence to confront untamed territory, and the Puritans specifically, with their passion for a triumph over matter by spirit, set in motion an implacable urge to spiritualize nature. Robinson inherited and perpetuated this urge, which had already built up considerable momentum, but history had altered the circumstances under which it could be obeyed. Art had replaced the church as the means to an original relation with the universe; in its powers, not those of doctrine, lay the keys to the divine. By luck of talent, Robinson was born in the temple of art; but by the misfortunes of time Christianity could no longer support him in his devotions. To transform the wilderness into civilization, the brute into a man, matter into spirit, he found it necessary to follow the lead of Emerson and others toward a non-theological religion. His poetry, as was natural for that in the Emersonian tradition, is a religious poetry, its motive in this respect being revealed explicitly by his remark about looking for the right blocks to spell God. When he wrote, ". . . J. and I are reading up . . . on Oriental Religions. I have been interested to find out that Christianity is in reality nothing more than Buddhism humanized," [40] he linked his sense of the religious with that of Emerson and the Transcendentalists, who preferred quoting Eastern religions to Christianity. Such a link was inevitable:

161

once the act becomes supreme, the divine becomes inseparable from what is and enters into the world process, or is that process, emerging ever anew as it creates from within out. Robinson's poetry is itself a contribution toward achieving the naturalistic religion he proclaimed to be known to science and prophesied to be on the way. Though all its original trappings have disappeared, the urge to etherealize the gross, to exalt in the spirit's release from and triumph over what would imprison it, remains intact in Robinson's poetry, and its forward thrust is carried to new religious frontiers.

For Robinson, the presence of the divine in the world, the final answer to Descartes's dualism, does not satisfy the mind's hunger for absolute truth; it does not eliminate mystery; rather, it re-establishes and insists upon it. Whereas the vulgar forms Protestantism took in ethics simplify in order to justify property ownership or the profit motive, the poetry of the act accents the complexity of life. As happiness cannot be mechanically produced, as high spirits cannot be willed, so life cannot be forced, possessed, or explained. It just is, miraculously, a gift, an unpredictable explosive force from no one knows where. Life pulses between its poles, man sensing the contradictory pulls they exert upon him. There is no explanation, only the mystery of opposites dynamically interacting. What Robinson's poetry of the act reveals is that the moral and metaphysical, the human and divine, the inner and outer, power and form, are inextricably interrelated. It exists, as does man, on two planes simultaneously, at the junction of two different levels of being.

Robinson's achievement, his stature as a major American poet, it should now be abundantly evident, lies in the thoroughness and consistency with which he explored the being of poetry and man. From this results the profundity Henry Steele Commager admired, the "philosophical" depth and breadth which characterize Robinson's poetry. Despite his regard for the past, he boldly faced his twentieth-century questionings and apprehensions and made poetry out of the actual currents of thought and feeling during his time. What he aspired to as man and poet, and substantially achieved, is eloquently stated by William James at the end of his *Psychology:*

When a dreadful object is presented, or when life as a whole turns up its dark abysses to our view, then the worthless ones among us lose their hold on the situation altogether, and either escape from its difficulties by averting their attention, or if they cannot do that, collapse into yielding masses of plaintiveness and fear. The effort required for facing and consenting to such objects is beyond their power to make. But the heroic mind does differently. To it, too, the objects are sinister and dreadful, unwelcome, incompatible with wished for things. But it can face them if necessary, without for that losing its hold upon the rest of life. The world thus finds in the heroic man its worthy match and mate; and the effort which he is able to put forth to hold himself erect and keep his heart unshaken is the direct measure of his worth and function in the game of human life. He can *stand* this Universe. He can meet it and keep up his faith in it in presence of those same features which lay his weaker brethren low. He can still find zest in it, not by 'ostrich-like forget-fulness,' but by pure inward willingness to face it with those deter-rent objects there. And hereby he makes himself one of the masters and the lords of life. . . . Neither in the theoretic nor in the practical sphere do we care for, or go for help to, those who have no head for risks, or sense of living in the perilous edge. . . . We draw new life from the heroic example. The prophet has drunk more deeply than anyone of the cup of bitterness, but his countenance is so unshaken and he speaks such mighty words of cheer that his will becomes our will, and our life is kindled at his own.[41]

The qualities James enthusiastically urges here are the ones Robinson admired in the life and works of others, "the hard, human pulse" and "the sure strength that fearless truth en-dows." And they are the qualities that he sought to realize in himself and his work.

Because he could unflinchingly face the actualities of life as they bared themselves to him, he was rewarded with an insight into human life that encompasses almost everything Ex-istentialism has more recently called to our attention.[42] Existen-tialism, of course, has refined its terms and explored its ideas at greater length, but Robinson knew the unhewn experience from which they arise. He saw the distinctiveness of man; he saw the

163

irreconcilability of thought and being, or the absurd; he saw that the essential context of human life is the relation of man to man; he saw that static categories and institutions are inherently hostile to the creative impulse; he saw the threatening nothingness from which life has to be perpetually redeemed. He also saw that under circumstances in which there is no recourse to transcendental, traditional, or a priori forms of knowledge, value resides in the act. But, above all, what Robinson discovered, and what constitutes his strongest bond with the climate of thought and feeling now identified as Existentialism, is that man stands alone and free; that, in fact, he is doomed to be free; that in the twilight of absolutes, with the only certainty his immediate concrete experience, his life's value is his own doing. To exist, as Whitehead has somewhere said, is to have a degree of order, but for Robinson to live is also to aspire for the decreation of old and the creation of new order; it is to seek a novel encounter with reality and to bear stoutly the burden of endlessly creating; for only through creativity could his spirit's will to live indomitably defy all the tendencies toward death in nature and society and man himself, only by continuous creative activity could his spirit resist inertia and keep from degenerating into matter. Appropriately, Robinson wrote poetry to his last day, editing proof for *King Jasper* on his death bed.[43] Poetry was indeed his life and his light.

Growth of Man—like Growth of Nature—
Gravitates within—
Atmosphere, and Sun endorse it—
But it stir—alone—

Each—its difficult Ideal
Must achieve—Itself—
Though the solitary prowess
Of a Silent Life—

Effort—is the sole condition—
Patience of Itself—
Patience of opposing forces—
And intact Belief—

Looking on—is the Department
Of its Audience—
But Transaction—is assisted
By no Countenance—

Emily Dickinson

NOTES

Key: SL *Selected Letters of Edwin Arlington Robinson,* ed. Ridgely
Torrence (New York, 1948).
US *Untriangulated Stars: The Letters of Edwin Arlington Robin-
son to Harry de Forest Smith, 1890-1905,* ed. Denham
Sutcliffe (Cambridge, Mass., 1943).

INTRODUCTION

1. "Poems of Experience," *Freeman,* V (April 19, 1922), 141-42.
2. Elizabeth Bates reports Robinson as saying that he was "perhaps
two hundred years in advance of his time" because of "his habit
of understatement, his absorption in the unconscious and semi-
conscious feelings and impulses of his characters . . . in which
he was unlike his contemporaries"—*Edwin Arlington Robinson and
His Manuscripts* (Waterville, Maine, 1944), p. 3. Despite the
exaggeration and dubious reason, the sentiment is genuine.
3. Studies by Yvor Winters, *Edwin Arlington Robinson* (Norfolk,
Conn., 1946), and Allen Tate, "Edwin Arlington Robinson,"
Collected Essays (Denver, 1959), pp. 358-65, are the only attention
the New Critics have given Robinson's poetry. Winters praises him
for not writing the kind of poetry the New Criticism favors, while
Tate criticizes him for failing to write that kind of poetry in his
late long poems. Both agree that Robinson's poetry is incompatible
with the taste of the New Criticism.
4. While some of the French symbolists, Whitman, and Yeats, for
example, have been frequently honored by their successors, Robinson
to my knowledge has been mentioned only twice by fellow poets,
once in Kenneth Rexroth's lines,

> What happened to Robinson
> Who used to stagger down Eighth Street,
> Dizzy with solitary gin?

Here it is significant that not his achievement or influence but his
disappearance is noteworthy.
5. Counting a generation every thirty years, with the year at the middle
point providing the generation with its title, and assuming the 20's as

a bench mark, the recent generations are the 1860's, the 90's, the 20's, and the 50's. Though inadequate in many ways for measuring recent historical eras, this rule-of-thumb device works reasonably well for discussing the intellectual history of the 100-year period from 1860 to the present in America. Finer distinctions can be made with decades or other units of time, but they are too fine for examining the larger sweep of ideas and attitudes germane to this discussion.

6. See, for example, Van Wyck Brooks, "The Silent Generation," *The Writer in America* (New York, 1953).
7. *Edwin Arlington Robinson* (New York), p. 30.
8. SL, p. 123.
9. *Irrational Man* (Garden City, N. Y., 1958), p. 29.
10. US, p. 254.
11. New York, 1960.
12. *The Massachusetts Review,* I (August, 1960), 609–30.
13. New York, pp. 15 and 17.
14. *The Necessary Angel* (New York, 1951), p. 117.
15. *Complete Poems of Robert Frost* (New York, 1949), p. 327.
16. *The Necessary Angel,* p. 140.
17. *The Necessary Angel,* p. 164.
18. *The Necessary Angel,* p. 154.
19. *Autobiography* (New York, 1951), p. 332.
20. *Selected Letters* (New York, 1957), p. 330.
21. *Poets of Reality* (Cambridge, Mass., 1965).
22. *The Next Development in Man* (New York, 1948).

CHAPTER I

1. SL, p. 166.
2. These phrases come, respectively, from Mark Van Doren, p. 30; Kaplan, *Philosophy in the Poetry of Edwin Arlington Robinson* (New York, 1940), p. 3; and Winters, p. 291.
3. *The American Mind* (New Haven, 1952), p. 160.
4. Karl Schriftgiesser, "An American Poet Speaks His Mind," *Boston Evening Transcript* (November 4, 1933), Book Section, p. 1.
5. SL, p. 111.
6. SL, p. 95.
7. US, p. 289.
8. US, p. 278.
9. "French Silence and American Poetry," *The Tradition of the New* (New York, 1959), p. 88.
10. George Santayana, "Three Philosophical Poets," *The Works of George Santayana* (New York, 1936-40), VI, 10. This is Santayana's definition of philosophical poetry.
11. *The Collected Poems of Edwin Arlington Robinson* (New York, 1937), p. 44. All quotations from Robinson's poetry are taken from this volume. Hereafter only the page number will be cited, and that will be given in the text immediately after the quotation.

12. Hermann Hagedorn, *Edwin Arlington Robinson* (New York, 1938), p. 370.
13. *Selections from the Letters of Thomas Sergeant Perry* (New York, 1929), pp. 3-4.
14. SL, p. 65.
15. SL, p. 160.
16. "Robinson to Moody: Ten Unpublished Letters," *American Literature* XXIII (May, 1951), p. 184.
17. *E. A. R. and His Manuscripts* (Waterville, Maine, 1944), p. 22.
18. SL, p. 170.
19. New York, 1930, p. 135. "In fact," Robinson wrote of Cestre's book, "he says a great deal that I have been waiting for someone to say—not only praise, which in itself doesn't always amount to much, but simple statements of what I have been trying to do" (SL, pp. 161-62).
20. "Edwin Arlington Robinson," *Bookman*, LXXV (November, 1932), 675–81.
21. US, p. 109.
22. SL, p. 113.
23. SL, p. 15.
24. SL, p. 13.
25. SL, p. 92.
26. SL, p. 165.
27. *East and West* (New York, 1956), p. 13.
28. SL, pp. 163-64.
29. SL, p. 160.
30. *Letters of Thomas Sergeant Perry*, p. 4.

CHAPTER II

1. US, p. 296.
2. SL, p. 172.
3. SL, p. 112.
4. Hagedorn, p. 311.
5. *The Letters of Hart Crane, 1916-1932*, ed. Brom Weber (New York, 1932), p. 238.
6. *Ibid.*, p. 237.
7. *Varieties of Religious Experience* (New York, 1923), pp. 498-99.
8. New York, 1914, p. 164.
9. *The Thought and Character of William James*, briefer version (New York, 1954), p. 214.
10. *Ibid.*, p. 209. The italics are Perry's.
11. *The Will to Believe and Other Essays in Popular Philosophy* (New York, 1919), p. 82. The italics are James's.
12. Robert D. Stevick, "Robinson and William James," *The University of Kansas City Review*, XXV (1959), 293-301. In this essay Mr. Stevick, while admitting that no external evidence exists, argues for the direct influence of James's ideas on "The Man Against the Sky." It is clear by now, I am sure, that my discussion assumes a pro-

nounced relation between Robinson and James, but whereas Mr. Stevick is concerned with influence (which undoubtedly occurred, and perhaps in both directions, for each knew the works of the other), I am concerned with the way Robinson thought through the problems of life via poetry and defined poetry in doing so. I draw parallels between Robinson and James to illuminate this matter.

13. *The Complete Works of Ralph Waldo Emerson*, centenary edition (Boston and New York, 1903), III, 74.
14. "Mathematics and the Good," *The Philosophy of Alfred North Whitehead*, 2nd ed. (New York, 1951), p. 557.
15. A. O. Lovejoy, *Revolt Against Dualism* (Chicago, 1930), p. 1.
16. Morton White, *Social Thought in America* (New York, 1949).
17. *Consciousness and Society* (New York, 1959), p. 66.
18. Quoted by Hughes, *ibid.*, p. 428.
19. *Revolt Against Dualism*, p. 7.
20. "My Mental Development," *The Basic Writings of Bertrand Russell*, ed. Robert E. Egner and Lester E. Denonn (New York, 1961), p. 40.
21. *Art as Experience* (New York, 1934), p. 22.
22. *Essays in Radical Empiricism* (New York, 1922), pp. 40 and 91.
23. *The Will to Believe*, p. 14.
24. *Ibid.*
25. *The Thought and Character of William James*, p. 277.
26. *Essays in Radical Empiricism*, p. 23.
27. *Ibid.*, p. 42.
28. This is Morton White's phrase (*Social Thought in America*, p. 24) for describing the reaction of Holmes, Dewey, and Veblen to nineteenth-century British empiricism. They, too, favored a radical empiricism.
29. *Revolt Against Dualism*, p. 55.
30. *Science and the Modern World* (New York, 1947), p. 107.
31. These are Lovejoy's words (p. 151), and they reveal that the historicism of the nineties, the sense of how ideas are related to temporal experience, affected even his vigorously abstract, logical mind.

CHAPTER III

1. SL, pp. 12-13.
2. "A Light exists in Spring," *The Complete Poems of Emily Dickinson*, ed. Thomas H. Johnson (Boston, 1960), p. 395.
3. SL, p. 177.
4. The phrase is C. E. M. Joad's, *The Recovery of Belief* (London, 1952), p. 33.
5. US, p. 160.
6. US, p. 212.
7. US, p. 175.
8. US, p. 158.
9. US, p. 134.

10. SL, p. 127.
11. SL, p. 139.
12. SL, p. 104.
13. SL, p. 165.
14. *Literature in the Making* (New York, 1917), p. 266.
15. Oxford, 1934.
16. *Autobiographies: Reveries Over Childhood and Youth and the Trembling of the Veil* (London, 1926), p. 176.
17. *Ibid.,* p. 233.
18. *Letters of Thomas Sergeant Perry,* p. 7.
19. US, p. 4.
20. US, pp. 213-14.
21. Princeton, 1953.
22. *Opus Posthumous* (New York, 1957), p. 166.
23. The difference between prose and poetry has been a prominent aesthetic question for some time now. Recent attempts at isolating what distinguishes them tend to be based on the schism between the objective and subjective, intellect and emotion. Herbert Read, for example, says, "If the thought is of a discursive or speculative origin, with creation or feeling subsumed or induced within its framework, then the form of expression is prosaic; if the thought is of an immediate or intuitive origin, if it is 'essentially vital,' but nevertheless assumes order and harmony, then the form of expression is poetic"—*English Prose Style* (London, 1928), p. 138. A more famous distinction is that made by Ogden and Richards, in *The Meaning of Meaning* (New York, 1959), between scientific and emotive language, but they go too far in making the two kinds of thought or language completely antithetical. Read is closer to the truth, and he is also closer to Robinson's understanding of the matter. Thus the difference between prosaic and poetic realism is a matter of emphasis, the first favoring the objective over the subjective, intellect over emotion, and the latter reversing the emphasis. Though decidedly objective and intellectual, Robinson's primordial source and ultimate commitment are the "subjective" and emotional.
24. *Introduction,* p. 22.
25. Laura E. Richards, *E.A.R.* (Cambridge, Mass., 1936), p. 8.
26. US, p. 135.
27. *Autobiographies,* p. 430.
28. SL, p. 50.
29. *Letters of Thomas Sergeant Perry,* p. 6.
30. *Dairy and Letters of Josephine Preston Peabody* (Boston and New York, 1925), p. 131.
31. US, p. 282. Robinson's remark was, "Zola is the greatest worker in the objective the world has ever seen."
32. US, p. 180.
33. US, p. 289.
34. New York, 1954, p. 13.

35. This is C. S. Lewis' phrase for describing the use made of love allegory by poets in the Middle Ages. *The Allegory of Love* (London, 1936).
36. US, p. 109.
37. SL, p. 67.
38. *E.A.R. and His Manuscripts,* p. 27.
39. US, p. 196.
40. US, p. 132. On another occasion he said, "There is poetry in all types of humanity—even in lawyers and horse-jockeys—if we are willing to search it out; and I have tried to find a little for the poor fellows in my hell, which is an exceedingly worldly and transitory one. . . ." (US, p. 108).
41. *E.A.R. and His Manuscripts,* pp. 8-9.
42. SL, p. 102.
43. Chicago, 1934, p. 6.
44. *English Language and English Poetry,* pp. 114-29.
45. Elizabeth Sewell, *Paul Valéry: The Mind in the Mirror* (New Haven, 1952), p. 24.
46. "The Symbolism of Poetry," *Essays and Introductions* (New York, 1961), p. 163.
47. US, p. 278.
48. Charles Beecher Hogan, "Letter to Edna Davis Romig," *A Bibliography of Edwin Arlington Robinson* (New Haven, 1936), p. 185.
49. Cf. Robert Langbaum, *The Poetry of Experience* (New York, 1957).
50. SL, p. 30.
51. William James employs this phrase to designate the location of the ideal, religious elements in experience (*Varieties of Religious Experience,* p. 73).

CHAPTER IV

1. In addition to being a literary theme, the conflict between individual and community treated in "Captain Craig" was a deeply disturbing personal problem for Robinson, because as Hermann Hagedorn remarks, "In his diffidence, as a man Robinson tacitly accepted the standards which, as a poet, he vehemently rejected, and judged himself by them. . . . He became obsessed by what, rightly or wrongly, he believed Gardiner thought of him" (Hagedorn, pp. 87-88). Robinson indicated the degree to which Gardiner was much on his mind when he said of it: "it . . . makes me positively sick to see the results of modern materialism as they are revealed in a town like this . . . we need local idealism . . . I wonder if a time is ever coming when the human race will acquire anything like a logical notion of human life. . . ." (US, p. 260). This is only one of many displays of this obsession in his letters. He repeatedly refers to his home town and townsmen critically, and he anxiously returns over and over again to the subjects of money, his vocation, and success.

Sorely plagued by the pressure Gardiner exerted upon him, he exclaimed, while a young man, "Business be damned" (US, p. 4). Yet later, as a successful poet, he made a point of itemizing his income from poetry, evidently pleased to measure his success by conventional standards (SL, p. 157). The itemization could have been meant ironically, but that is of no consequence; Gardiner never left him in peace.

2. These terms, which I will rely upon somewhat heavily hereafter, are George Herbert Mead's, in *Mind, Self and Society.* Their meaning can be extracted from the following passages: There are "the selfish versus the unselfish sides or aspects of the self . . . the relation between the rational and primarily social side of the self and its impulsive or emotional or primarily anti-social and individual side" (p. 230). "The possibilities in our nature, those sorts of energy which William James took so much pleasure in indicating, are possibilities of the self that lie beyond our own immediate presentation. We do not know just what they are. . . . The possibilities of the 'I' belong to that which is actually going on, taking place, and it is in some sense the most fascinating part of our experience. It is there that novelty arises and it is there that our most important values are located. It is the realization in some sense of this self that we are continually seeking" (p. 204). "The 'I,' then, in this relation of the 'I' and the 'Me,' is something that is, so to speak, responding to a social situation which is within the experience of the individual. It is the answer which the individual makes to the attitude which others take toward him when he assumes an attitude toward them. Now, the attitudes he is taking toward them are present in his own experience, but his response to them will contain a novel element. The 'I' gives the sense of freedom, of initiative. The situation is there for us to act in a self-conscious fashion. We are aware of ourselves, and of what the situation is, but exactly how we will act never gets into experience until after the action takes place" (pp. 177-78).

3. US, p. 260.
4. *The Collected Works,* I, 73.
5. *Irrational Man,* p. 4.
6. *Edwin Arlington Robinson,* p. 51.
7. Nancy Evans, "Edwin Arlington Robinson."

CHAPTER V

1. This is the opinion of Yvor Winters, *op. cit.*
2. *E.A.R. and His Manuscripts,* p. 22.
3. SL, p. 168.
4. "The Art of Fiction," *The House of Fiction,* ed. Leon Edel (London, 1957), pp. 23-45.
5. Hagedorn, p. 338.
6. *Ibid.,* p. 175.

7. From an unpublished letter to John Drinkwater, dated November 23, 1927, in the Houghton Library at Harvard.
8. SL, p. 113.
9. *Mind, Self and Society*, p. 204.
10. *Webster's New Collegiate Dictionary* (Springfield, Mass., 1953).
11. *Introduction*, p. 142.
12. *Literature Considered as Philosophy* (London, 1957), p. 25.
13. *The Complete Works*, III, 65.
14. US, p. 141.

CHAPTER VI

1. Unpublished letter of Robinson's to Mrs. Lionel Marks, dated November 17, 1919, in the Houghton Library.
2. *Edwin Arlington Robinson*, p. 340.
3. *The Works of George Santayana*, X, 248.
4. *The Octopus* (New York, 1928), III, 343.
5. *Introduction*, p. 138.
6. *The Collected Works*, I, 76.
7. SL, p. 93.
8. Quoted by Stanley K. Coffman, Jr., in *Imagism: A Chapter for the History of Modern Poetry* (University of Oklahoma, 1951), p. 90.
9. *The Letters of Ezra Pound, 1907-1941*, ed. D. D. Paige (New York, 1950), p. 6.
10. Coffman, p. 12.
11. Winters, p. 144.
12. Stanley Coffman quotes the following poem by H. D.:

Whirl up, sea—
Whirl your pointed pines,
Splash your great pines
On our rocks
Hurl your green over us.
Cover us with your pools of fir.

He comments, "The principal material of her early poems is an intensely concentrated reaction to some natural object, a reaction that is always evoked by the object as a physical thing" (*Imagism*, p. 147). Of course, the reaction is a human emotional response, but what makes this an Imagistic poem, and a good one, is that though the object as physical thing, intensely seen, becomes symbolic of the human condition, the superhuman proportions of the sea, the metaphor of the rock, and the plural pronoun leave man a victim of overwhelming natural forces acting upon adamant substance. In such a world "we" long to be bathed by or dissolved in the cool tranquillity of death, that being the only escape of the spirit from materiality or objectivity.
13. This is Pietrim Sorokin's term, in *The Crisis of Our Time*, to designate the empirical character of modern Western culture.

14. *Imagism*, p. 63.
15. Richard Buchminster Fuller, *Time*, LXXXIII (January 10, 1964), 46-51.
16 *The Meeting of East and West* (New York, 1946), p. 311.
17. F. S. C. Northrop, working with this idea at a time when it had become well established, said of science and art: "The true relation between intuitive, aesthetic, and religious feeling and scientific doctrine is one of mutual supplementation. For we have a conception of the meaning of man and the universe which it is trustworthy for art and religion to convey only by the aid of scientific knowledge pursued to its basic theoretical assumptions, and thus developed to its philosophical and theological consequences. And conversely, we can attain verified scientific knowledge only by observing what is immediately apprehended, and this is always aesthetically vivid and emotionally moving" (*The Meeting of East and West*, p. 63).
18. SL, p. 169.
19. *Rococo to Cubism in Art and Literature* (New York, 1960), p. 258.
20. *Autobiography*, p. 335.
21. Quoted by Sypher, p. 265.
22. New York, 1911, p. 209.
23. Wallace Stevens, drawing on Simone Weil, defines decreation as "making pass from the created to the uncreated (destruction is from the created to nothingness)," *The Necessary Angel*, p. 174.
24. This phrase is adapted from Alfred North Whitehead, *Modes of Thought*, and is cited by Wallace Stevens in *The Necessary Angel*, p. 115.

CHAPTER VII

1. *American Poetry Since 1900* (New York, 1923), p. 66.
2. "Poems of Experience."
3. *Introduction*, p. 14.
4. Bliss Perry, *New York American*, April 22, 1931.
5. US, p. 93.
6. SL, p. 49.
7. *The Complete Poems of Emily Dickinson*, ed. Thomas H. Johnson (Boston, 1960), p. 365.
8. *The Philosophy of George Santayana*, ed. Irwin Edman (New York, 1936), p. 590.
9. SL, p. 137.
10. Hagedorn, p. 332.
11. *Plays and Controversies* (New York, 1924), p. 122.
12. *Paul Valéry*, p. 11.
13. The phrase is Oscar Kokoshka's; quoted by Herbert Read in *A Concise History of Modern Painting* (New York, 1959), p. 244.
14. New York, 1915, p. 140.
15. US, p. 97.
16. SL, pp. 17-18.

17. *Opus Posthumous*, p. 243.
18. *The Complete Works*, I, 134.
19. *Edwin Arlington Robinson*, p. 263.
20. *American Poetry in the Nineties*, pp. 1-72.
21. *Opus Posthumous*, p. 244.
22. SL, p. 168.
23. This is the way thinkers around the turn of the century were inclined to speak about the relation of the inner and outer world. William James, for example, said, "As concrete states of mind, made up of a feeling *plus* a specific sort of object, religious emotions of course are psychic entities . . ." (*Varieties of Religious Experience*, p. 28); and again, ". . . every philosophy should be touched with emotion to be rightly understood" (*ibid.*, p. 433). See also the passage quoted from Santayana's *Three Philosophical Poets*. Objects and ideas can be abstracted out of experience until, as in science, they have no human relevance; then, if they are to be significant for man or an individual, emotion has to be turned upon them. Given the dichotomy between subject and object, meaning and value enter the world through man's contribution of a subjective element to his experience. Even though radical empiricism was designed to break down this dichotomy, semantic habits forced James and others to speak in its terms.
24. *The Letters of Thomas Sergeant Perry*, p. 10.
25. *The Necessary Angel*, p. 174.
26. *Tragic Sense of Life*, p. 124.
27. *Ibid.*, p. 119.
28. *The Works of George Santayana*, VI, 67.
29. *Bernard Shaw: Complete Plays With Prefaces* (New York, 1962), III, 600.
30. *Art as Experience*, p. 20.
31. *The Complete Works*, I, 90.
32. *Ibid.*, I, 4.
33. *Ibid.*, I, 96.
34. To see how deep and pervasive the hold of voluntarism on the American mind is today, one need only think of Wallace Stevens' notion of the poem as an act of the mind, or of Kenneth Burke's notion of literature as "equipment for living"; of the American style in painting (some say it is America's first original contribution to this art) known as "Action Painting"; of Jack Kerouac's and Charles Olson's notion of spontaneous writing, which locates the significance of literature in the act of writing; of the academic criticism of Louis Martz and Earl Wasserman, who read poems as acts; of the interest in Zen Buddhism, particularly Zen art, for which value resides in the artistic performance; and of the aesthetic theory of Paul Ziff, who, quoting Chinese philosophers as authorities, is trying to account for the "meaning" of art on the basis of the aesthetic experience as an act ("Reasons in Art Criticism," *Philosophy and Education*, ed. Isaac Scheffler [Boston, 1958], pp. 219-36). The

poetic and intellectual tradition which Emerson initiated and pragmatism formally articulates represents the major sustained effort of the American to make sense of his experience; and as he has done so he has repeatedly acknowledged that, for him, to be is to act, and to act is to be. What he knows, what is real for him, is rooted ultimately in activity, in making and doing, in continual becoming.

35. *The Works of George Santayana,* VI, 24-25.

36. I take naturalism in Santayana's sense and realism as I defined it in Chapter III to differ only in emphasis, in that the former primarily refers to a concept of reality and the latter to the epistemology of the same philosophical view. Here, however, Santayana is talking about the methodology of naturalism, so his remarks are for the most part also true of realism.

37. Robinson remarked, for instance, about Tristram: "The fool potion, or philtre, in the Tristram story has always been an incurable source of annoyance to me, and after fighting it away for four or five years I have finally succumbed to telling the story of what might have happened to human beings in those circumstances, without their wits and wills having been taken away by some impossible and wholly superfluous concoction. Men and women can make trouble enough for themselves without being denatured and turned into robots" (SL, p. 145). And again, "That damn dose has always spoiled one of the world's greatest stories and probably will continue to do so" (SL, p. 146).

38. New York, 1955, pp. 333-34.

39. *Selected Letters,* p. 297.

40. US, p. 274.

41. P. 400.

42. For a fuller examination of the parallels between Robinson and Existentialism see Richard Crowder, "E. A. Robinson and the Meaning of Life," *Chicago Review,* XV (Summer, 1961), 5-17. Though Crowder is too much concerned with Robinson's "so-called philosophy," his essay does properly establish and enlarge the context in which Robinson's poetry must be viewed to be correctly understood.

43. Recent factual evidence supporting this statement appears in Harold S. Latham's *My Life in Publishing* (New York, 1965), where Mr. Latham recalls that Robinson came out of a coma to deliver the promised manuscript of *King Jasper,* then relapsed and died a few hours later.

INDEX